BREATHE

BETTER

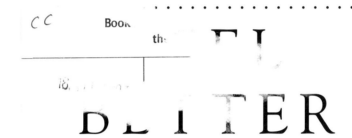

BREATHE
BETTER

· ·

FEEL
BETTER

*Learn to increase your
energy, control anxiety and
anger, relieve health problems,
and just relax with simple
breathing techniques*

Howard Kent

APPLE

CONTENTS

A QUARTO BOOK

Published by the Apple Press
6 Blundell Street
London N7 9BH

© Copyright 1997 Quarto Publishing plc

ISBN 1-85076-948-6

This book was designed and produced by
Quarto Publishing plc
The Old Brewery
6 Blundell Street
London N7 9BH

Typeset by Central Southern Typesetters,
Eastbourne
Manufactured in Hong Kong by Regent
Publishing Services Ltd
Printed in China by Leefung-Asco Printers
Ltd

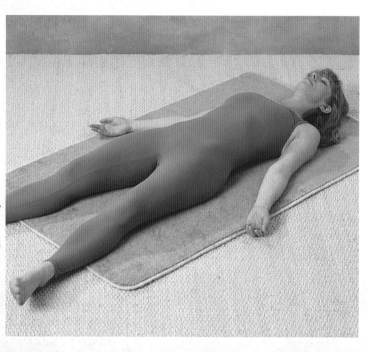

LEARNING TO BREATHE AGAIN

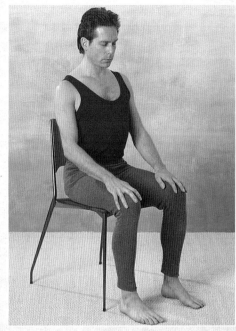

PREFACE

Concern is growing – and rightly so – about the way we are polluting Planet Earth and the serious repercussions that this is having on our health. Much of this pollution directly affects the atmosphere, resulting in our breathing in harmful substances. However, while we are arguing about the steps necessary to overcome this alarming situation, we have to keep on breathing! Our breathing normally need not be deep, but it must be free – free from fear, agitation, and all negative feelings, because these very emotions harm the whole respiratory process.

Pollution, we need to remember, is not only man-made; nature itself has provided many environmental challenges to the human race and will continue to do so. It is for this reason that our nasal organs have built-in cleansing and purifying processes. Harmful particles are trapped in the cilia, a host of tiny hairs in the nose, that act as pollution traps. The breathing process also adjusts the temperature of the air automatically. Properly used, these safeguards are of inestimable value to us.

It becomes clear that the normal, natural process of breathing is through the nose. Breathing in through the mouth is an emergency system and should always be regarded as such. Even vigorous physical activity can usually be achieved more efficiently while breathing in through the nose, though an out-breath through the mouth will not be harmful. Breathing in through the mouth bypasses nature's health safeguards and becomes a hazardous process.

But even breathing in through the nostrils will produce problems if accompanied by harmful thoughts. We have two respiratory centers in the brain which control the in- (sympathetic) and out- (para-sympathetic) breaths. These centers respond to a whole range of sensors – heat or cold, as one example; equally, peacefulness or tension. The result is that the body's psychophysical system either functions in a free and relaxed manner or it is put on a damaging "red alert."

A few million years ago, a relative handful of our ancestors lived on this planet, surrounded by awesome predators and faced with constant challenges from the forces of nature. Now most of the predators have died out, and there are some five billion human beings! Compared with so many other creatures that the planet has produced, we humans seem fragile but, in fact, we have an enormous inborn strength. We live in a permanent state of self-awareness that, when used for our development, is of incalculable value but when we use this form of consciousness to encourage doubts, fears, anger, frustration, and other negative impulses, it becomes destructive.

This does not mean that there is no place in our lives for these harmful impulses, but their value is to acknowledge them and then to rise above them – not to let them continue to eat our heart and our health out.

So we can – and should – be angry at the way our planet and the air we breathe are being polluted, but that anger should lead to a quiet determination to play our part in opposing these evils. Our strength to do so will, to a large degree, depend upon the freedom of our breath – linked to a mental steadfastness of purpose. Simply to blame others for our wrongs, building up our own tensions and blockages, is both useless and harmful.

The aim of this book is to free our breathing, free our thoughts – and, consequently, to free our lives.

INTRODUCTION

If you live to be 80, you are likely to have taken somewhere in the region of 630 million breaths during your lifetime. (People normally breathe around 15 times per minute.) Each breath is a moment of life, a renewal of life in every sense, and we are aware that we only have to stop breathing for three minutes or so to be dead.

The Bible tells us that God breathed the breath of life into Adam. Every civilization has paid homage to the breath. The yoga sages of India declared, "Breath is life. Life is breath." Yet we know little about the whole process of respiration; this process is far wider and more subtle than we realize. The expression, "Breath is life," is not limited to human beings or even to creatures with lungs. Trees breathe, and we have come increasingly to understand that their respiratory process is linked intimately with our lives. In its full sense, respiration is the process of being, lying at the very heart of the concept of ecology.

What do we mean by breathing? Clearly the use of the gaseous content of the atmosphere around our planet is central to human life, yet this is but one part of a complex process upon which not merely our existence, but also our well-being within that existence, depends. Respiration may therefore be defined as the interrelation of many of the forces that make up existence. One of these universal forces is that of electromagnetism. We know, for example, that our planet has its own electromagnetic field, which is in a constant state of interplay with other such fields. The concept of Gaia, or the living planet, has evolved from this knowledge.

BALANCING OXYGEN AND CARBON DIOXIDE

Human beings tend to concentrate on the relationship of oxygen and carbon dioxide through the functioning of the heart and the lungs as being the whole process of breathing. Yet even here there is much confusion. Breathing exercises in many books and articles urge us to empty the lungs completely, failing to realize that even if we could do so, the result would be catastrophic, because the lungs would then collapse. In fact after the deepest of out-breaths some 1,600 ml. of air will remain in the lungs, while after a normal out-breath the figure is some 2,900 ml.

Both oxygen and carbon-dioxide are essential to us. Often we are led to believe that oxygen is the wonderful life-giving substance, while carbon dioxide is a nasty poison. In fact, too much oxygen can be as harmful as too little and, in this area, the basis of effective breathing is to provide a natural balance between the two gases and to ensure the free flow of the oxygen through the body. Too much emphasis is placed on deep breathing, which can often become forced and strained. We may drive an automobile capable of reaching 120 miles per hour, but rarely do we attempt such a speed, not simply because of legal limits, but also because of the wear on the engine and other working parts. The capacity to breathe deeply is important, but in most situations it is the free flow of the breath that matters more than its depth.

SHALLOW BREATHING

One of the most common problems in our society is shallow breathing. This involves rapid respiration, using the top of the lungs, and is quite different from a moderate free breath. While there are some medical experts in this field, all too often the significance of shallow breathing is overlooked, ultimately with serious results. The process that we call hyperventilation can be a response to many challenges: emotional, environmental, and physical. As a result of such challenges, there is a tendency to take small breaths – a sign of unease with life – using only a small upper part of the lungs. Here, because of the constant effect of the force of gravity, the exchange of gases becomes more difficult and the oxygen level drops. To compensate the breath speeds up and then, in turn, the carbon dioxide level is reduced. The result is a series of disturbing symptoms, including dizziness, irritability, and excessive sighing.

The fact that such shallow breathing also inhibits the movement of the diaphragm – the body's piston – producing more health problems, including tension in the heart area and ineffectual functioning of the vital organs in the abdomen, has not yet been sufficiently researched.

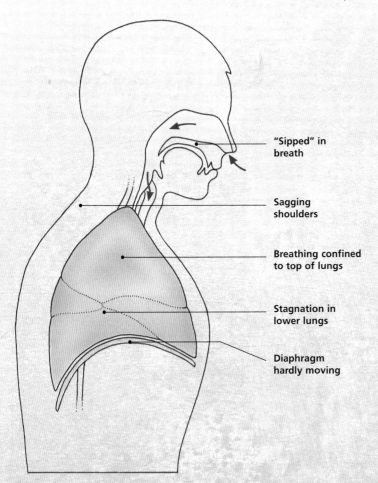

"Sipped" in breath

Sagging shoulders

Breathing confined to top of lungs

Stagnation in lower lungs

Diaphragm hardly moving

EFFECTIVE DISTRIBUTION OF OXYGEN

We need to recognize that respiratory areas situated in the brain constantly monitor the breathing process: fear inhibits the in-breath; anger produces a panting breath; pain seizes up the breath altogether. These are the more dramatic effects, but the response to lesser challenges will also impede the natural flow of body energy. Natural and effective breathing is not a process of increasing the intake of oxygen, but of securing its effective distribution. In fact, when we are quiet and peaceful, the body's oxygen intake is reduced because the breathing slows down. From an average of 15 breaths per minute, when we relax effectively or move into a state of meditation, the rate drops to around six breaths a minute, with a decline in oxygen intake of up to 10 percent.

We know that such states, as one important aspect of our lives, stimulate health and effective body functioning. What in fact happens is that a state of physical and mental peace results in a freer flow developing within the body. Wastage of oxygen energy, which occurs when we are tense and strained, is reduced dramatically. As one example experiments have shown that circulation in the muscles increases by up to 300 percent in the state of meditation.

A BABY'S BREATHING

Another common misconception is that adults should breathe like babies, but respiration during the first year or two of life is very different from that of an older child or adult. The human baby comes into the world in a less complete state than any other species. Bones are soft and strengthen gradually – whereas a foal or calf is standing within minutes of birth, it takes a baby many months to achieve this. It is also around a year before the coating on the central nervous system (the myelin sheath) is complete.

In addition, the baby's brain is receiving and storing countless impressions to prepare it for a full human life as the process of self-awareness develops. The baby breathes not at the rate of 15 breaths per minute, but at 50! As adults, the nearest we come to the baby's style of breathing is while we sleep, when, we believe, a mental-sifting process goes on (partly to be seen in our dreams) and body-repair activities are promoted.

The psychophysical development of the baby brings about natural changes in the breathing process. The processes of physical coordination and verbal expression are instinctive. Without external urging, the baby "knows" it needs to control its arms and legs; also that its storehouse of impressions is now capable of communication through distinctive sounds.

As this happens the breathing rate slows markedly and the rapid abdominal movements are replaced by the use of the intercostal muscles to draw out the lower ribs on the in-breath, so the diaphragm – the strongest sheet of muscle in the body – is stretched, moving down on the inhalation and resuming its cone-like shape on the out-breath. This pumping motion is at the core of

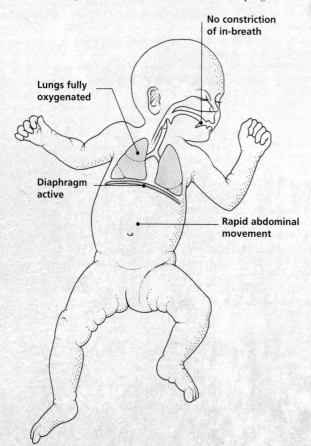

No constriction of in-breath

Lungs fully oxygenated

Diaphragm active

Rapid abdominal movement

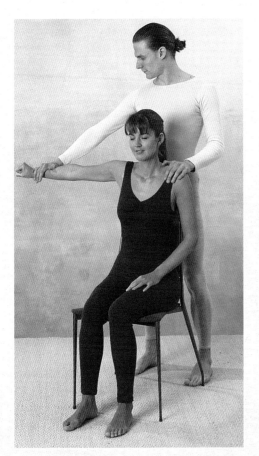

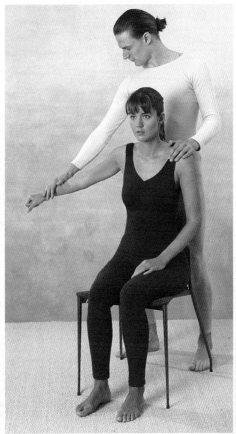

the body's total flow of energy, while also stimulating the heart and the abdominal organs. As the baby begins to use the intercostal muscles, the abdominal movement stops whenever energy is required either for physical or specific mental activity.

EXPLODING A FALLACY

The belief that we should continue to inflate the abdomen on the in-breath is still widespread, both among doctors and even many teachers of yoga breathing techniques. A leading Indian research institute, Kaivalyadhama, which has been investigating breathing for many years, has exploded this fallacy. The founder of the institute, Swami Kuvalayananda, has written "The Western physical culturists advise their followers to draw out the abdomen at the time of inhalation. In our opinion this is due to some wrong conceptions about the physiology of deep breathing. They appear to be under the

impression that they can admit a larger quantity of fresh air and consequently of oxygen, if they were to draw out their abdomen. But in the laboratory evidence that we have collected . . . we have found this to be an error of judgment. The fact is that the controlled abdomen allows at the time more oxygen to be inhaled than the protracted abdomen. So far as the culture of nerves is concerned, controlled abdominal muscles have a decided advantage over protracted abdominal muscles . . ."

The truth of this statement can be checked easily. On pages 22–3 details of a simple arm muscle test are given. Follow this by checking the tone of one arm first of all. Then take a half dozen deep breaths, letting the abdomen expand on the in-breath. Now check again, and it will be found that the muscles have become markedly weaker. Now take another half dozen breaths, ensuring the abdomen is controlled and only the bottom ribs expand. It will now be seen that muscle strength is much greater than it was originally.

THE BASIS OF VITALITY

Over the centuries human beings have sought to discover the basis of vitality. Special attention to breathing has marked many of the major civilizations. The ancient yogis of India paid little attention to the functioning of the lungs, realizing that if we used the body naturally and lived a calm, controlled life, the effective use of oxygen would follow. Instead, they concentrated their attention on a flow of energy through the body through what they called the *Nadis*, usually translated as the subtle nervous system.

Before this idea is dismissed as rubbish, it is worth pointing out that a distinguished British medical researcher, Sir Charles Shillington, had a paper published in the *British Medical Journal* as long ago as 1930, claiming he had discovered a fine, web-like network throughout the human body. This would appear to correlate with the *Nadis* of the yogis and the meridians of Chinese acupuncture. More research is needed, but does not appear to be taking place.

Ancient yogis claimed that an energy system, called the Nadis, permeated the whole body. It is now known that the human nervous system contains an electrical current which appears to support this belief.

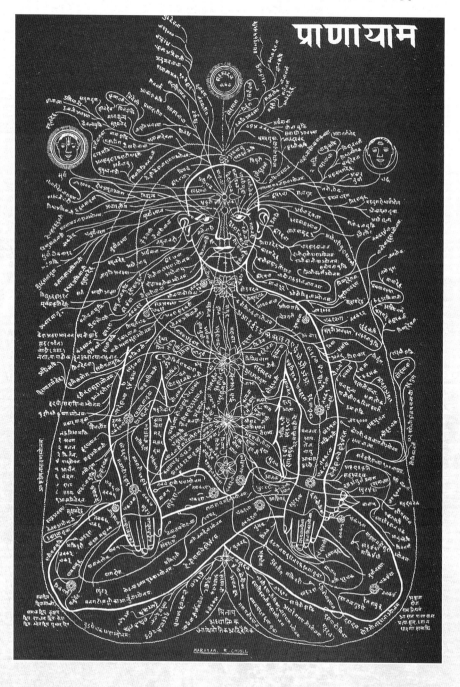

ELECTROMAGNETISM

More recently research has been undertaken into the body's electromagnetic system. Many interesting facts have emerged, but we are still a long way from a thorough understanding of the subject. One outstanding researcher of the subject was the late Professor Harold Saxton Burr, of Yale University, who established the fact that every human cell has its own electrical field. He called the totality of these the Life-field, or L-field for short. He also postulated that deficiencies or damage within this field must have an intricate connection with ill health.

Within the last 25 years, an understanding has grown of the role electricity plays in maintaining and repairing bone structure. As a result the stimulation of bone growth and repair by electric therapeutic treatment is now common in hospital practice. However, is such external stimulation necessary? Our lives are most determined by personal experiences, and I must relate one of my own at this point.

When I was in my early sixties, I was working with someone suffering from severe ataxia (intention tremor). Suddenly his head was affected and his forehead, out of control, crashed against my cheekbone, fracturing the xygomotic arch. I drove to the emergency room of the local hospital, where X rays confirmed the damage. I was offered an operation, which I declined, and instead took two days off and concentrated on my breathing. I then returned to my center where I was working with a doctor from St. Bartholomew's Hospital in London.

We were working with disabled people, using a machine which checked the body's electrical field. Becoming the patient, I submitted myself to a test, which showed that the electrical flow in the area around the fracture was very low. It appeared to be generated naturally, but was rapidly being used up. The deduction was that this force was needed to assist in the repair of the fracture. I then spent five minutes breathing quite deeply, controlling the abdomen and visualizing the energy flowing into the fracture to repair it. Another test with the machine showed a remarkable heightening in the electrical field around the fracture.

Aboriginal artists showed an aura round the human body. Recent research reveals this is an electrical field, sometimes called the "coronary discharge."

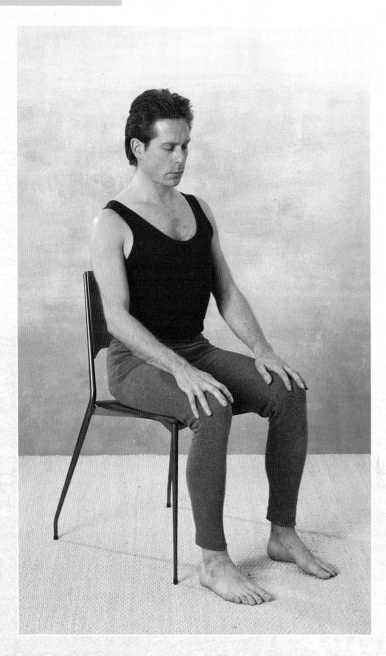

A comfortable upright position allows the flow of breath to be free and the trunk to function naturally.

directly affect the way we breathe: Controlling our breath will have an impact on the way we think.

I must provide one further personal experience. In the 1980s I was flying back at night from conducting a training course in Barbados when we flew into a tropical storm. Suddenly the captain spoke to us – 300-plus people in a jumbo jet – on the intercom. He said that the crew had been trying to check a persistent alarm signal from the main cargo hold. Their efforts had been in vain, and it had to be treated as an emergency. He had arranged for us to land in the Azores, but it would take about 30 minutes to reach there.

Naturally this announcement concentrated our minds! Such things happen only to other people, never to us. After a few minutes, although I could see signs of deep concern around me, I suddenly wondered why I felt alert but remarkably calm. Then the thought, "How are you breathing?" came to me. I discovered that I was automatically breathing in precisely the way I had been teaching: quite deeply, slowly, and with substantial intercostal movement. We landed eventually and were hurried down the emergency chutes in a gale and torrential rain. I still felt alert and, above all, controlled. Twenty-three people were injured, three becoming stretcher cases, while I suffered no ill effects.

While it is good to know how important the linking of mind and breath will be in an emergency, it is the less dramatic daily happenings that are of the greatest importance. We are told that a constant drip of water will wear away a stone. The constant disregard of breathing constrictions and problems caused by facing life's daily challenges in the wrong way can, in due course, be equally damaging.

Never forget these interlinked factors: that breath is life and that we have remarkable control over our breath. Properly used the control of breath *is* the control of life.

Within 10 days the problem was over: no operation, no artificial electrical stimulation. There has been no trouble since, although many medical professionals, even today, would declare that the bones of someone of 60-plus must already be weakening.

When we consider that it is clear that the thoughts of human beings have a direct link with the body's functioning, it becomes obvious that this amazing process we call respiration is of immense importance to us in every aspect of our lives. Our thoughts

DO'S AND DON'TS

We human beings all too often tend to tackle our problems either with grim determination or intermittently, excusing ourselves for our lack of purpose. Success, however, demands a balance: an understanding that regular practice is essential, but that working in a strained manner will defeat our objective.

This need for balance applies when putting into practice the suggestions offered in this book. The central message is that breathing is a natural process, but that, to be effective, our lives must also be lived naturally, both posturally and mentally. This, then, is a day-by-day – almost minute-by-minute – approach and one that initially requires care and attention. Overcoming poor mental and physical habits is a slow process. It is a cliché to say that we get out of life what we put into it, but remember a cliché is a truth that we tend to disregard.

The majority of the ideas suggested in this book can be carried out in regular everyday circumstances. They will not require special clothing or surroundings. They will require total concentration, even if only for two or three minutes. Never let these practices become purely notional, for when we exclude mental control, we are ignoring the most important element.

Try, at the end of each day, to go over what has happened and how you responded. This will help considerably in ensuring regular practice. Some of the ideas put

forward are more formal yoga postures or variations on a yoga theme. For these comfortably loose clothing should be worn and the practice carried out either on a special mat or on suitable carpeting. The atmosphere should be as dust free as possible. No serious body exercise should be done for at least two hours after a meal, otherwise you will impede effective digestion.

The lungs particularly need to be treated intelligently. Pollution, smoking, and mucus can block the passages, and these blockages need to be approached with care. In most cases practice will clear the lungs, but the old adage, "Not too little; not too much," applies. Practice should be constant but not forced. Where more severe damage, such as emphysema, has occurred, gentleness is the order of the day. Never forget that quiet practice, linked with a firm, calm mental state, can work wonders.

If in doubt be sure to consult your physician or a qualified therapist in whom you place your trust. Remember, though, that in many ways you are your best physician; become aware of what your body and mind are telling you. The messages will be clear if you are quiet and listen to them. These messages will also tell you what activities to increase, as well as those needing greater gentleness.

As you get in touch with your breath, you get in touch with life itself; it is a wonderful and rewarding experience.

Nasal strips have recently become a popular way of increasing nasal airflow, particularly for snoring and during sports. However, they have only a short-term effect and should not be considered in the same light as the long-term breathing improvements covered in this book.

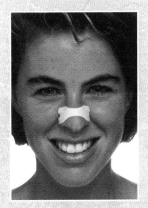

HOW TO USE THIS BOOK

We are constantly offered all sorts of ways to enhance our lives. There are countless exercise programs. Books and courses offer us advice on how – and indeed what – to think. Diets come and go in the hundreds. Many of these suggestions will have value, yet we may not pursue any of them and still live to a ripe old age. A woman in France who recently celebrated her 121st birthday gave up smoking when she was 117 and confessed to still having a passion for chocolates.

However, although we can ignore our breathing, we cannot do without it. Some 2,000 years ago, the sages who devised the science of yoga declared, "The life breath is pure consciousness." If we regard breathing as simply an automatic process, our lives undoubtedly will be impaired as physical and mental strains and stresses arise. The joy for humans is that breathing is also a voluntary process, enabling us to take a degree of control over life itself.

Central to the evolution of the human being is the desire – perhaps we should say, the need – to achieve. This arises from the fact that self-awareness is a focal part of our lives. Sadly, this need to achieve is all too often encouraged merely in material terms, when clearly it goes much further than that. Millions listened when Frank Sinatra sang, "I did it my way."

The purpose of this book, therefore, is to underline how a knowledge of the inter-relationship between our breath and our minds can develop a real sense of achievement, leading to better health, a more peaceful approach to life, and enhanced relationships with others. That great sage, the Buddha, declared some 2,500 years ago, "Set your heart in one place and nothing is impossible to you." He also taught the art of conscious breathing. He emphasized, therefore, that a clear sense of purpose – for "set" means "make firm" – combined with a worthy objective – hence the word "heart" – can produce amazing results.

This book combines fundamentals and practical tips. The fundamentals naturally lie

at the very basis of our lives and from these how consciously we make use of the breath of life will develop. Many of the tips will overlap, and it is only possible in a single volume to provide a number of "for instances." For example, one section deals with various aspects of health breakdown, but in each instance only one or two specific suggestions can be offered. The book as a whole, though, will provide the basis of a program offering a wider approach to individual problems. By following its precepts it offers the opportunity of incorporating into daily life a variety of simple actions which

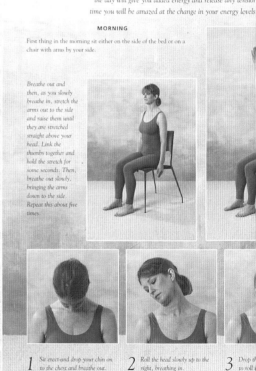

LEARNING TO
BREATHE AGAIN
42

ENERGIZE YOUR

BREATHING PROGRAM

Spending a few minutes on simple breathing techniques at r the day will give you added energy and release any tension time you will be amazed at the change in your energy levels

MORNING

First thing in the morning sit either on the side of the bed or on a chair with arms by your side.

Breathe out and then, as you slowly breathe in, stretch the arms out to the side and raise them until they are stretched straight above your head. Link the thumbs together and hold the stretch for some seconds. Then, breathe out slowly, bringing the arms down to the side. Repeat this about five times.

1 Sit erect and drop your chin on to the chest and breathe out.

2 Roll the head slowly up to the right, breathing in.

3 Drop t to roll breathing times in each

Exercise shown in step-by-step sequence.

can enhance our mental approach and, in turn, stimulate the body's resistance to ill heath and degeneration.

We are conditioned to be told what to do, what medication to take, what therapeutic program to undergo – in other words to abrogate our responsibility. This book deliberately avoids such an approach; to use the book effectively, it is best to read it all through first. Then, since many of us have now become accustomed to working with programs, one good way of using the book is to devise a program that suits you personally. This can be written down briefly with a note of the relevant page numbers. Always remember that this is a throughout-the-day approach and not merely a brief exercise program which can be performed and then ignored. Such an approach also encourages flexibility, which is important because in a number of ways our needs vary as life progresses, and different aspects may need to be emphasized. Mapping out your own program clearly gives virtually limitless opportunities, rather than restricting you to a step-by-step approach. This book should be a companion through life and not merely one to be relegated to the bookshelf.

LEARNING TO
BREATHE AGAIN
43

NOON

Many people now spend a considerable portion of the day sitting, or in a position which tends to seize up the muscles. To ease this tension, sit in a chair and do the following exercise.

1 Link the hands behind the back of the chair, breathe out, and then, as you breathe in, push the chest out and raise the linked arms as high as possible. Relax as you breathe out slowly.

2 After doing this five or so times, sit comfortably upright with the hands together in the lap and breathe slowly and gently for a couple of minutes. Repeat this during the day whenever you start feeling stiff.

NIGHT

Just before going to bed, do the stretch you did in the morning, to ease the muscles and then lie for a few minutes either on the bed (if it is not too soft) or on the floor with the legs apart and arms away from the sides, palms upward. Close the eyes, breathe gently and slowly. To calm down mind and body, now let the stomach rise and fall with the breath – but do not force it, let the movement be natural. Maintain for three to five minutes.

43

1 •————————— *Number of chapter for easy reference.*

If a technique has been explained earlier in the book, a single picture is shown as a reminder and you should refer back to the original explanation.

Read the instructions carefully before trying out the exercises, until you are confident that you can remember them correctly. Every so often it is worth re-reading the text to make sure that no errors have crept into your routine.

BREATH – AND YOUR ENERGY

FROM BABY TO ADULT

During the first months of life, one of the brain's main tasks is to store billions of sensory impressions – sounds, color, taste, touch, smell. At the same time, the body is being "finished off" – bones are setting, the cover on the nervous system (myelin sheath) is being completed and many other physical developments are taking place. At this stage babies breathe quite rapidly, with the abdomen moving up and down.

Big changes take place between the ages of one and two. A child learns to walk and coordinate arms and legs and distinguish sounds, leading to language. This results in a change in the breathing process. The inter-costal muscles begin to pull the bottom ribs up and out as the child breathes in, straightening the strong sheet of muscle – the diaphragm – which is attached to them in the front and to the spine at the back. At this stage the child's breathing differs very little from that of an adult. Increasingly, the trunk functions as a pump, with the vigor of the pumping motion depending on the mental and physical activities being undertaken.

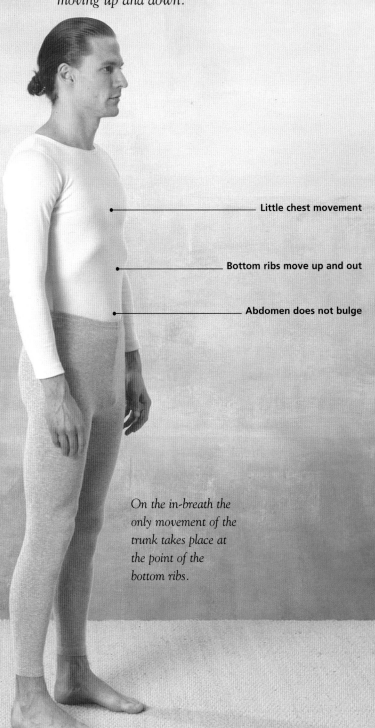

Little chest movement

Bottom ribs move up and out

Abdomen does not bulge

On the in-breath the only movement of the trunk takes place at the point of the bottom ribs.

THE BODY'S PISTON

The body is a "whole energy system," of which one vital part is the lungs, constantly balancing the intake of oxygen and carbon dioxide. Equally important is the body's electromagnetic flow, for every cell in the body has a tiny electrical field that connects to the central "life force."

When you breathe out, the diaphragm has a cone-like shape in the middle of the trunk.

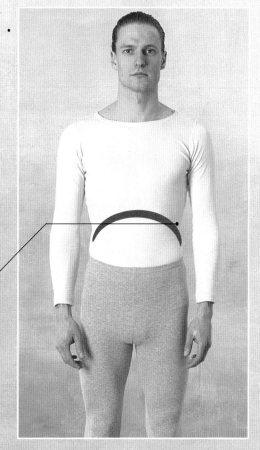

Cone-like shape of diaphragm on out-breath

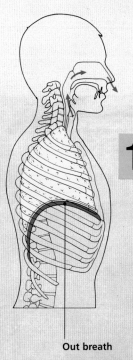

Out breath

1

When you breathe in, the principal movement takes place at the position of the lower ribs, and the diaphragm straightens according to the depth of the breath. The stomach does not inflate, creating a system of internal pressure on the inhalation and relaxation on the exhalation – a pumping movement. At the same time, the motion of the diaphragm also ensures that the lungs are used fully.

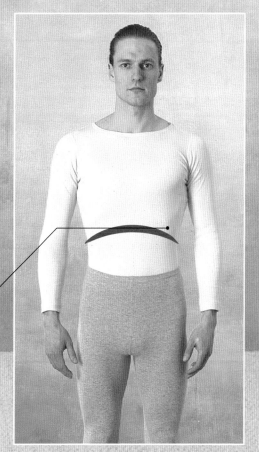

Diaphragm straightens as in-breath pulls bottom ribs up and out

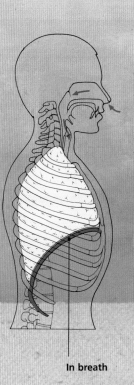

In breath

RHYTHM OF LIFE

UNDERSTANDING RESPIRATION

Respiration is an intricate process, not confined to the lungs and oxygenation. It is also the basis of energy generation, linked directly with the pumping of the heart and the two interlinked rhythms – breathing and heartbeat.

Respiration is truly the "rhythm of life." Compare it with a great orchestra playing a symphony: the beat will vary according to the mood; there will be separate rhythms among the different sections, in harmony with the central beat. The orchestra *can* play on its own, but for a truly balanced performance it needs a conductor. You have control of the way you breathe and, in doing so, can improve your feelings of energy. But you need to understand the process first.

To breathe in, you tense the muscles of the trunk, drawing the air in through the nostrils. At the same time the lungs expand and, combined with the muscular tension, this creates effective pressure in the chest. Similarly, the descent of the diaphragm, with the light control of the abdominal wall, stimulates equivalent abdominal pressure.

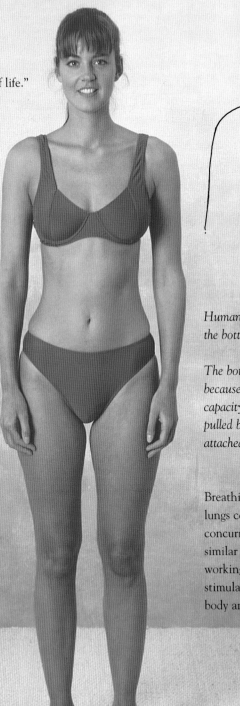

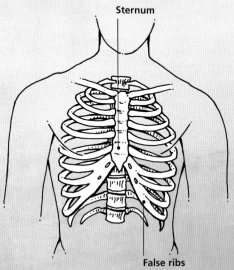

Human trunk, showing the rib cage and how the bottom ribs come up to join the sternum.

The bottom ribs (called the "false ribs") because of their unique formation, have the capacity to move up and out as you breathe, pulled by the intercostal muscles that are attached to them.

Breathing out, all the muscles relax and the lungs contract, releasing the tension. The concurrent rising of the diaphragm has a similar effect abdominally. Thus the lungs are working effectively, but the process also stimulates the flow of energy throughout the body and the body's electromagnetic field.

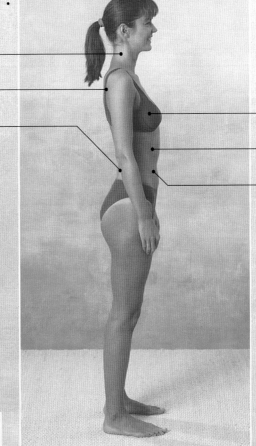

Balanced neck and
shoulder muscles

Erect spine

Balanced back
muscles

Rhythmical massage
of heart

Diaphragm free
to move

Abdominal organs
massaged

1

Human posture did not develop by chance. It
is part of an evolving design. When the trunk
is comfortably upright, the spine and the
muscles are correctly balanced, the diaphragm
is able to function as a piston, and the
interplay between tension and relaxation
creates the necessary harmony for effective
bodily function. This harmony is conveyed to
the brain, via the nervous system, and plays
its role in stimulating a peaceful mental
outlook. The picture on the right
demonstrates good posture while those below
show the effects of bad posture.

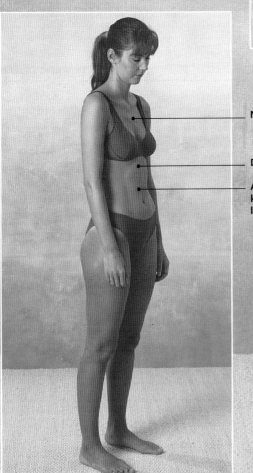

No heart massage

Diaphragm "stuck"

Abdominal organs
kept under pressure
leading to stagnation

Constant tension

Diaphragm movement
restricted

Abdominal area tense

Back muscles
under pressure

BRAIN AND BODY

YOU ARE WHAT YOU THINK

Human lives are lived in a state of self-awareness: constantly relating to others and to circumstances. Human thought process is dominated by this and it is very hard to be dispassionate. You are happy when people like you, when the sun is shining, when there is money in the bank. You are unhappy when you feel you are disliked, when it is cold and wet, and when you are broke. Your emotional state affects your body, including the way you breathe, constantly.

The interrelationships between brain and body are virtually total. As you breathe, so your mental attitude either stimulates or retards the functioning of your body. Research has shown the dramatic physical consequences that can follow the state of unhappiness known as unrelieved stress. You can check how your attitude affects your body quite easily by trying this experiment. You will need a friend to help.

One hand on the wrist

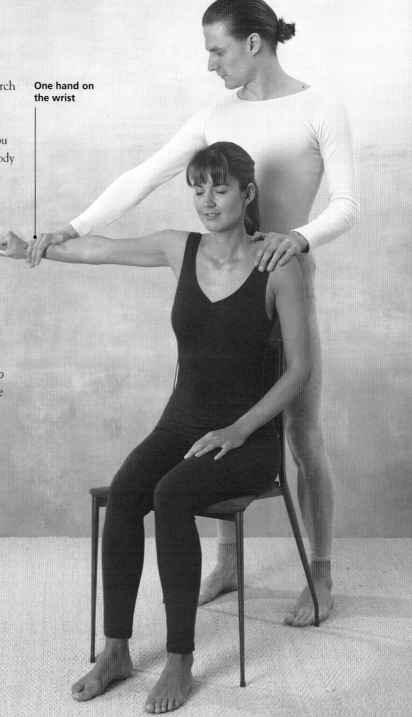

1 Sit comfortably erect in a chair and extend one arm to the side. Clench the fist and tense the muscles. Get your friend to stand behind you, one hand on your opposite shoulder and the other on the wrist of the extended arm. Then, with a firm pressure, your friend tries to push the arm down, checking the tone of the muscle.

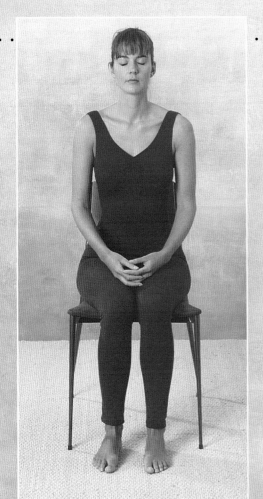

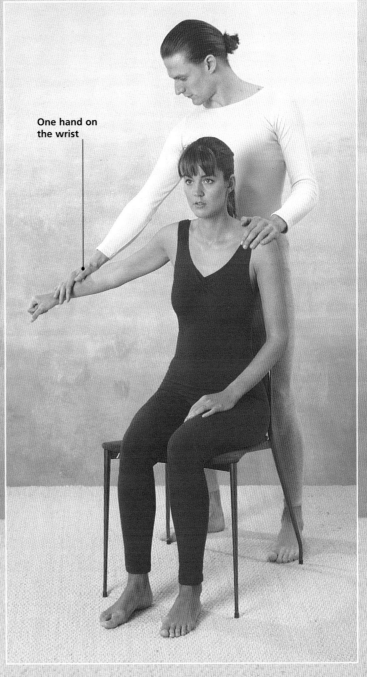

**One hand on
the wrist**

1

*2 Sit quietly for a couple of minutes,
thinking either of something that makes
you happy, or of something that makes you
unhappy. Concentrate on that single thought,
keeping to the emotion you have chosen.*

*3 Now get your friend to check the muscle
tone of the same arm again. If your
thought was a happy one, the tone will have
strengthened. If it was unhappy, the tone will
have weakened considerably.*

*If, having done this
test, you feel it is too
subjective, try it on
someone who has no
idea of its purpose.
The result will be
exactly the same.*

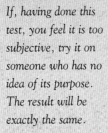

LEARNING TO RELAX

RELAXATION AND BREATHING

*A baby's fast abdominal breathing – up to 50 breaths a minute – is specific to the
functions it is having to perform. Self-awareness emerges slowly as the brain is
flooded with sensory impressions. When we – conscious – adults relax, our
breathing does not speed up, instead it slows down.*

For adults to relax they need a period of quiet
observation: observation without
interference. This is extremely difficult to
achieve because brain impressions – unbidden
thoughts – crowd in, causing both mental and
physical "disease." If, however, you give in to
this flood of impressions, you are creating the
human equivalent of keeping an engine
running continuously – your body will
overheat, wear out, and break down. The
ability to relax, therefore, is central to a
healthy life. The most effective way to train
yourself to relax is to lie on your back on a
warm, draft-free carpeted floor and to follow
the guidelines shown.

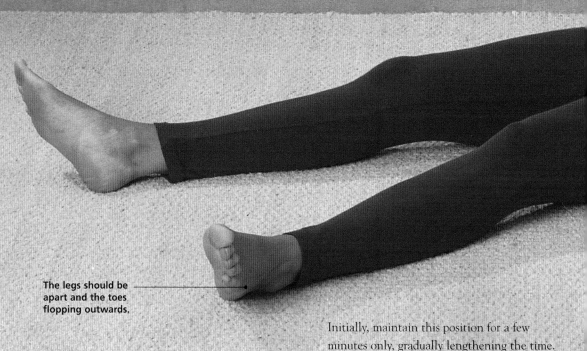

The legs should be
apart and the toes
flopping outwards,

Initially, maintain this position for a few
minutes only, gradually lengthening the time.
Remember, you cannot try to relax, it has to
come naturally. Observing the slow and
rhythmical nature of the breath will help to
improve your natural breathing generally.

1

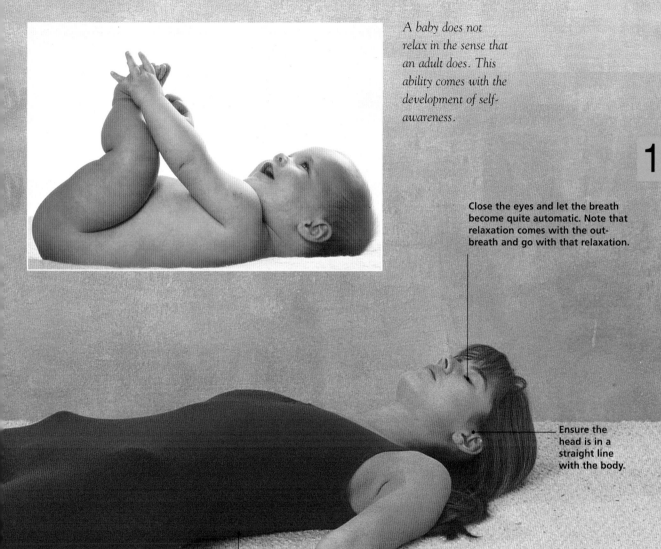

A baby does not relax in the sense that an adult does. This ability comes with the development of self-awareness.

Close the eyes and let the breath become quite automatic. Note that relaxation comes with the out-breath and go with that relaxation.

Ensure the head is in a straight line with the body.

The back should lie comfortably against the ground.

The arms should be away from the sides with the hands limp and the palms upward.

If you want to think a pleasant, peaceful thought, do so, or visualize a calming color. If unbidden thoughts intrude – they will! – let them flow away again gently. Slowly, but surely, they will diminish. Because you are letting go, the abdomen rises gently as you breathe in and, as you breathe out, it falls – a slow, gentle, natural movement. So long as you remain aware of this, you will be relaxed but will not fall asleep. Sleep and relaxation are two different things.

REST, RELAXATION
AND SLEEP

LETTING GO

It is easy to confuse relaxation and sleep. While relaxing you retain consciousness, while the aim of sleep is to lose it. In one form or other, relaxation or sheer tiredness will lead to sleep, but the unique benefits of relaxation stem from its role of peaceful observation.

Research suggests that important factors in your sleep patterns include internal body repair and a review of memories, leading to dreams. There is no doubt, too, that stresses and fears usually play some part in the sleeping process. Hence you can have what appears to be a good night's sleep and

yet still feel tired and jaded. The body slows down during sleep, its temperature drops, and breathing becomes shallow. When you dream, the specific energy required for the process brings the heartbeat near to the collapse rate and breathing becomes a pant.

Relaxation is often confused with "slumping." However, as shown on page 21, a slumped posture interferes both with breathing and with natural body function, so the "slump" is certainly not beneficial.

If you have learned to relax by lying down effectively, you will soon find that sitting comfortably erect is much more beneficial than just letting the body flop.

RELAXING INTO SLEEP

It is sensible to train yourself to lie on your back in bed, even if only for a short time, bringing the mind to bear on a gentle, quite slow breath. The breath of sleep is more thoracic than abdominal – that is, the movement is higher up in the lungs – so do not attempt to breathe deeply or move the abdomen. Do, however, let the concept of quiet, slow harmony and rhythm dominate.

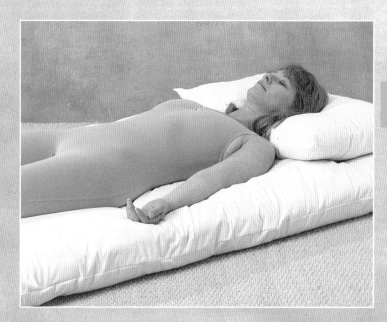

1

Most people have positions they naturally assume in bed and there is no reason to change these. Plant the idea of calmness and harmony firmly in your mind, so that if you wake during the night, you will find you bring the breath under control automatically.

Consciousness of the breath is also important on waking up in the morning. Again, a few minutes lying on your back will help, combined with a slow, rhythmical breathing pattern, paying special attention to a feeling of relaxation on the out-breath.

PRONE TO TENSION

THE NECK AND SHOULDERS

*Certain parts of the body are more susceptible to tension than others; the neck
and shoulders are prime examples of this. Even if you have a fairly relaxed
attitude to life, these are vulnerable parts of the body. The resulting
strains can not only promote mental agitation (and irritation) but also advance
actual ill-health.*

As you grow older, the ability to turn your
head from side to side tends to get less. This
can be countered effectively by combining
movement and breathing as shown.

1   *Looking to the front, cup the right hand
under the chin and place the left hand on
the back of the head, toward the right side.
Breathe in and, as you breathe out, gently but
firmly push the chin to the right, keeping the
head upright. Hold your final position and then
move back slowly, breathing in.*

2   *Reverse the hands, with the left hand cupping the chin, and repeat
the process, again linking with the breath.*

3   *Finally, bring both hands on to the back
of the head. Breathe in and, as you
breathe out, press the chin firmly on to the
chest, stretching the back of the neck.*

FREEING THE MUSCLES

1

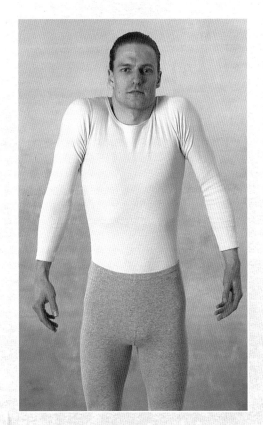

1 Brief, but effective, tension relief can be obtained by shoulder-shrugging. Breathing in, shrug the shoulders as close as possible to the ears. As you breathe out, let them drop down.

Make this a swift movement, dropping rather than lowering the shoulders.

2 Single shoulder-shrugging is also useful, alternating the shoulders. This, too, is performed with the in-breath on the shrug and the out-breath on the drop.

If you find one side stiffer than the other, pay it special attention.

SPINAL STRENGTH

THE CAT

Much is written about how to keep the spine and back in good order, but while slight reference is sometimes made to breathing, it is generally regarded as insignificant and therefore often overlooked. When you appreciate that the state of both the neuromuscular system and the mind are closely related to the way you breathe, you will realize that effective breathing is not just an optional extra but enhances oxygenation of the blood and stimulates mobility.

1 The yoga asana (posture) for the back called the Cat wholly links movement and breath to great benefit. Get onto all fours, the knees a little apart, level with the hips and the hands parallel with the shoulders. Having first breathed out, breathe in slowly and deeply as you bring the lower back down, opening the chest and raising the head. Hold this posture for a few seconds.

2 Breathing out, arch the back as high as possible, bringing the head down. Again hold between movements. Repeat a number of times, always letting the steady flow of the breath direct the movement.

3 Finally, sink forward on the knees, until the forehead touches the ground (or as nearly as possible), and bring the arms parallel to the side, with the hands, palms upward, by the feet. Breathe in a gentle, relaxed fashion and hold for a minute or two.

THE VALUE OF "WIGGLING"

It is noticeable that people who live in a
warm climate are more supple than those
living in colder countries. The stiffness
brought on by cold weather can be very
harmful and can be counteracted with this
simple exercise.

*1 Stand with the feet a little apart, hands
on hips and simply "wiggle." Breathe in
as the "wiggle" opens the chest and out as it
reduces it.*

1

**This should be a fun
movement not a
"serious" one.**

*2 Really let yourself go, moving in all
directions, as though you were keeping a
hula-hoop in the air. As the movement is quite
rapid, it is more difficult to link with the
breathing, but practice will help considerably
and the value of the exercise will therefore be
enhanced accordingly.*

There are many other effective movements to
benefit back and spine (some more are given
on pages 86–7). Once you experience the
pivotal role played by the breath, you will see
how important it is to make breathing central
to the whole process. A general rule is that
when tension is required, breathe in; when
relaxation takes place, breathe out. Where
the chest is opened, breathe in; where the
chest is contracted, breathe out.

**Stiffness is often
linked to inhibition –
so go fully into the
spirit of the
movement.**

BALANCE AND BREATHING

A MOVEMENT OF JOY

An eminent medical man once declared: "Nothing is purely physical and nothing is purely mental. Everything is psychophysical." Humans tend to think of balance as a part of their physical existence, yet, in fact, it is linked with the state of the mind and both are expressed through the breath.

1 *Stand with the feet a little apart, the arms relaxed but just away from the body in an "open" attitude.*

Always take your time – never rush the movement. Combine mental and physical calmness.

2 *Having breathed out, as you breathe in begin to stretch the arms out and up, not as a purely physical movement but as an expression of joy. Bring the arms stretched out parallel with the shoulders, with the palms upward, still experiencing this feeling of peace and openness.*

3 *Hold for a few seconds and then slowly bring the arms down again on the out-breath. Repeat several times.*

. . . .

STANDING – AND BREATHING – TALL

1 *This movement stimulates physical balance through mental balance. Stand, feet a few inches apart, and breathing in, bring the palms together in a prayer position on the chest. Close your eyes and bring a peaceful thought into your mind.*

1

3 *Finally, on another in-breath, stretch the arms high into the air, palms remaining together. The same peaceful thought remains. Come down in the same stages, the movement now on the out-breath.*

2 *Breathe out and, breathing in again, bring the hands, palms still together, onto the head. Retain the peaceful thought.*

TAKING CHARGE

CONTROLLING YOUR EMOTIONS

One can live without speech,

for there are the dumb.

One can live without sight,

for there are the blind.

One can live without hearing,

for there are the deaf.

One can live without thought,

for there are the simple.

One can live without limbs,

for there are the crippled.

But one cannot live without breath

— *Ancient Indian text*

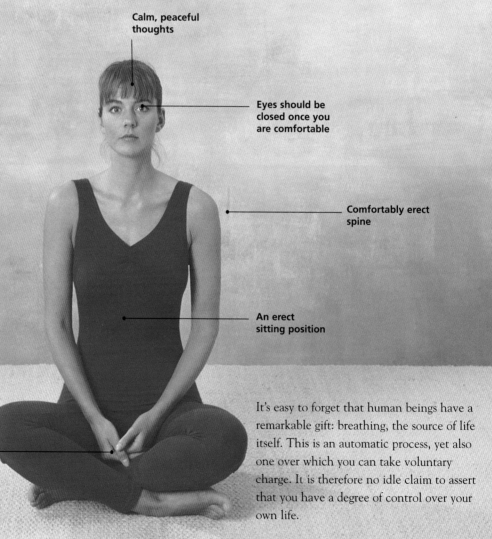

Calm, peaceful thoughts

A traditional sitting position can be helpful, but sitting in a chair can be just as effective: the vital thing is to have a comfortably erect spine – sitting-up rather than sitting-down. Then, with the eyes closed, breathe calmly and rhythmically. As one example, as you breathe in, say to yourself: "I breathe in life." As you breathe out: "I breathe out life." Just a few minutes spent in this way can produce a truly calming effect, enhancing both mental and physical processes.

Eyes should be closed once you are comfortable

Comfortably erect spine

An erect sitting position

Hands touching, resting on lap

It's easy to forget that human beings have a remarkable gift: breathing, the source of life itself. This is an automatic process, yet also one over which you can take voluntary charge. It is therefore no idle claim to assert that you have a degree of control over your own life.

1

Choose a still scene that appeals to you and hold it consistently in the mind's eye.

It is easy to recognize that calmness is always linked with a calm breath, and fear is linked with an agitated breath – in fact, whatever the emotion, the breath changes to emphasize it. Hence, it makes logical sense to accept that prolonged damaged breathing can precipitate ill-health and that all too easily a vicious downward spiral ensues.

The sages of the concept known as yoga (literally "oneness") realized that control of life and health depends upon calmness, dispassion, the ability to "take things in your stride" and to maintain a calm and free breathing process. This is why learning to sit quietly and to breathe correctly is of such great importance.

REALITY AND ILLUSION

. . . .

POWER OF THE HUMAN MIND

Nobody can define a border line between reality and illusion. In countless medical trials, placebos – sugar-coated pills of no value – have often produced better results in patients suffering from specific illnesses than the pharmaceutical product being tested. This demonstrates the remarkable power of the human mind. The breath responds to every emotion. It will be tense if you are insecure, and it will be free if you accept and feel peaceful.

While it is known that every breath brings gases into the body and that our lives depend upon an effective flow of oxygen, most people fail to realize that the body is also electromagnetic, with every cell having its own tiny electrical field and that this is linked directly with breathing. The presence of an electrical flow along the nervous system has been known for some 200 years. Now the electrical nature of the human heart is also understood, together with the fact that all body systems have a direct relationship with this universal force of energy. A simple way of checking this (see page 22) is the change in tone of the arm muscles directly in relationship to a state of mind.

STIMULATING THE FLOW OF ENERGY

A process of visualization can be used to stimulate the flow of all forms of energy through the body. Scientists use vegetable dyes in experiments to see how a flow occurs; we are using a similar mental process. Sitting erect, with the eyes closed, begin to breathe quite slowly and rhythmically. Imagine that the atmosphere you are drawing into the body is a warm, golden mist. Each time you breathe in, feel that the golden mist is rising to the very top of your head.

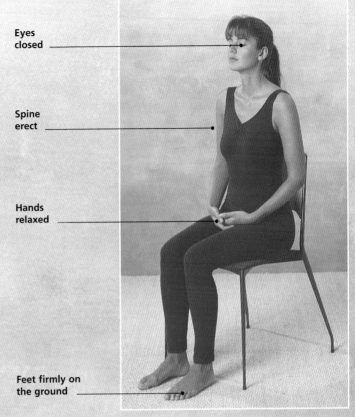

Eyes closed

Spine erect

Hands relaxed

Feet firmly on the ground

1

Sitting erect, with the eyes closed, begin to breathe quite slowly and rhythmically. Breathing out as slowly as you can, sense this golden mist flowing right down through the body into the fingers and toes. They will feel warmer and even begin to tingle. You are aware that this flow is passing through every part of your body.

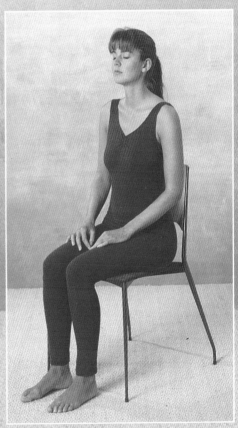

If you have special difficulties with some parts of the body, pay them special attention, but never lose sight of the fact that it is a flow affecting every part of you. As you get used to the process, you will be able to lengthen the time taken. Around 20 minutes of visualization can be extremely beneficial. Not only will you have a feeling of well-being and enhanced energy, but the whole body will be toned up and the immune system will be stimulated.

BANISHING DEPRESSION

· ·

THE CONSCIOUS SELF

The link between your mental outlook and your physical body needs to be emphasized, for it is all too easy to understand something theoretically and much harder to deal with it practically. A wise old woman once remarked: "I've had a lot of problems in my life and most of them never happened!" It is amazing how many perceived problems can be cut down to size if you tackle them through breath and mind.

When you are feeling strong and happy, you are sure you can achieve all sorts of desirable things. Yet even quite a slight setback can destroy this confidence and you accept that you are trapped by your thoughts and by your weakened body. This is where you must remind yourself that your breathing – the very source of life – is substantially under your voluntary control. Physical and mental problems may impair the breath, but "I," the conscious self, has the capacity to take over.

Depression and tension tend to bring about hyperventilation. Instead of using all your lungs when breathing, thus ensuring an effective flow of oxygen, you use only the top (clavicular) area. Because of the force of gravity, gas exchange is more difficult in the top part of the lungs; the oxygen level drops and, automatically, the breath speeds up to combat this, resulting in too great a discharge of carbon dioxide. This enhances the mental depression, creates irritation and weakens the functioning of the whole body.

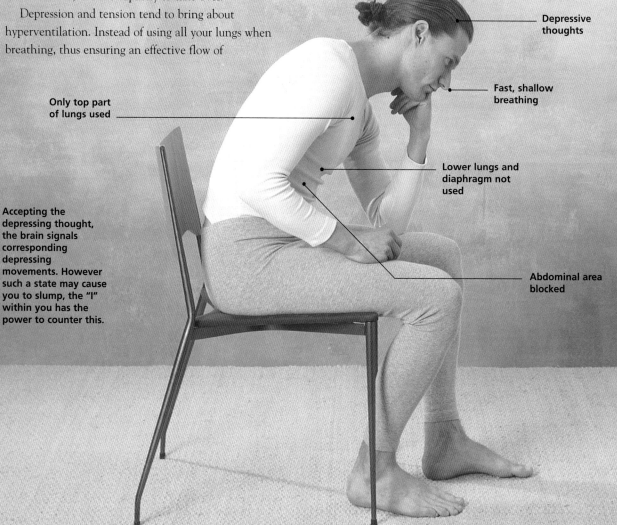

Depressive thoughts

Fast, shallow breathing

Only top part of lungs used

Lower lungs and diaphragm not used

Accepting the depressing thought, the brain signals corresponding depressing movements. However such a state may cause you to slump, the "I" within you has the power to counter this.

Abdominal area blocked

MINIMIZING PROBLEMS

The two pictures both show clearly the differences that you can bring about by conscious action. Sit correctly with spine erect and your hands resting on your thighs. You will be surprised to find how difficult it is to remain depressed in this posture. Enhance this positive feeling by swinging the arms up in an attitude of exultation as you breathe in.

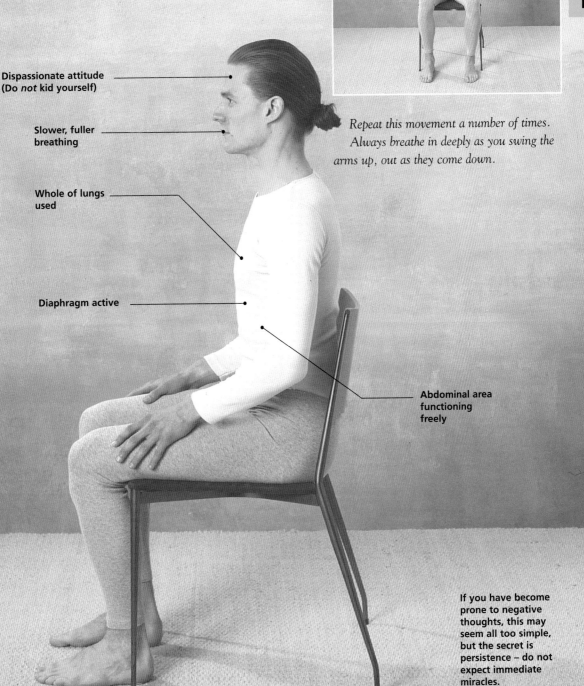

1

Repeat this movement a number of times. Always breathe in deeply as you swing the arms up, out as they come down.

Dispassionate attitude
(Do *not* kid yourself)

Slower, fuller
breathing

Whole of lungs
used

Diaphragm active

Abdominal area
functioning
freely

If you have become prone to negative thoughts, this may seem all too simple, but the secret is persistence – do not expect immediate miracles.

HANDLING STRESS

CHANGES IN BREATHING

There are times in life when you feel that you just cannot cope with all the pressures that are crowding in. Not necessarily just bad things, either! A "stress gauge," devised in the U.S., has shown that your health can be adversely affected by happy events, such as marriage or a new and more responsible job, if it seems as if there are too many things to do and think about at the same time.

As problems pile up, the brain takes in breathing changes, but these do not help you cope: they are only a response to the feeling of mental confusion, and matters will get worse until you make a conscious decision to bring the situation under control.

	1		2		3		4			1		2		3		4	
L	I	F	E		PAUSE		I	S	B	R	E	A	T	H

	1		2		3		4			1		2		3		4	
B	R	E	A	T	H		PAUSE		I	S		L	I	F	E

The first step is to make sure that you slow down. Firmly and deliberately, breathe slowly, saying to yourself, as you breathe in, "Life . . ." and, as you breathe out, ". . . is breath." Then "Breath . . ." and on the exhalation," . . . is life." Gently, but positively, push away any other thoughts. Mind and body will soon begin to feel the benefit.

1

One of the joys of consciousness is the ability to visualize. Of course, you can use this in the wrong way, letting images of gloom and doom harm you; but if you choose and hold onto the right imagery, you can bring about remarkable beneficial changes. Bring into your mind a blue summer sky, with a few little fluffy clouds. There is virtually no wind and the clouds are only just moving. You are sitting comfortably erect with your hands on your lap and your eyes closed, becoming absorbed by this peaceful scene. Your breathing will slow down in response to the picture you are creating, the muscles will relax and the body's energy will flow gently and effectively. As body and mind calm down, your ability to deal with the issues concerning you will be enhanced. Start with five minutes or so and build up slowly. Ten minutes should be quite sufficient.

ENERGIZE YOUR DAY

BREATHING PROGRAM

Spending a few minutes on simple breathing techniques at regular intervals during the day will give you added energy and release any tensions. Over a period of time you will be amazed at the change in your energy levels and general outlook.

MORNING

First thing in the morning sit either on the side of the bed or on a chair with your arms by your side.

Breathe out and then, as you slowly breathe in, stretch the arms out to the side and raise them until they are stretched straight above your head. Link the thumbs together and hold the stretch for some seconds. Then, breathe out slowly, bringing the arms down to the side. Repeat this about five times.

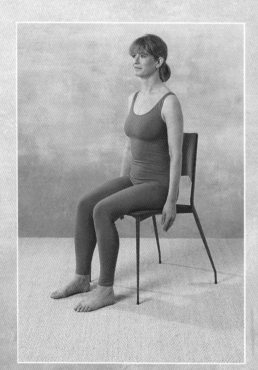

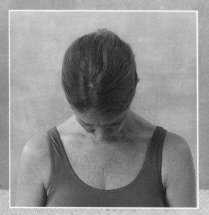

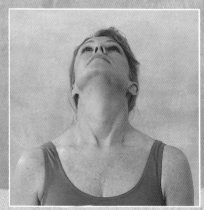

1 *Sit erect and drop your chin on to the chest and breathe out.*

2 *Roll the head slowly up to the right, breathing in.*

3 *Let the head drop back Do not force it back. Continue to roll it down to the left, now breathing out. Repeat three times in each direction.*

NOON

Many people now spend a considerable portion of the day sitting, or in a position which tends to seize up the muscles. To ease this tension, sit in a chair and do the following exercise.

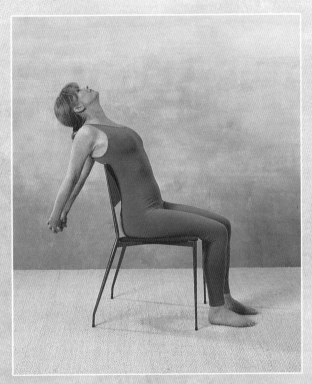

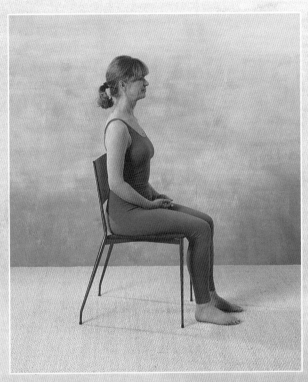

1 Link the hands behind the back of the chair, breathe out and then, as you breathe in, push the chest out and raise the linked arms as high as possible. Relax as you breathe out slowly.

2 After doing this five or so times, sit comfortably upright with the hands together in the lap and breathe slowly and gently for a couple of minutes. Repeat this during the day whenever you start feeling stiff.

NIGHT

Just before going to bed, do the stretch you did in the morning, to ease the muscles and then lie for a few minutes either on the bed (if it is not too soft) or on the floor with the legs apart and arms away from the sides, palms upward. Close the eyes, breathe gently and slowly. To calm down mind and body, now let the stomach rise and fall with the breath – but do not force the movement; let it be a natural one. Maintain for three to five minutes.

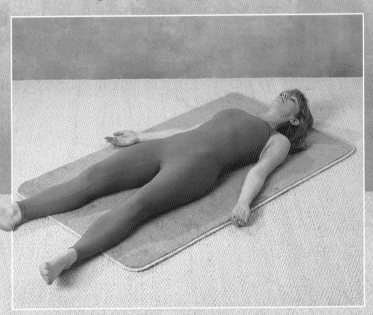

STOP SHIVERING

SENSORY RESPONSES

Humans spend much of their lives responding to what they perceive to be the messages of their senses: cold, heat, sounds, touch, taste and smell. But these are the responses they have become accustomed to make and they are quite subjective.

An Inuit flying into a temperate climate would find it intolerably hot. Someone from a tropical country would shiver. An inhabitant of such a land might say it was just comfortably warm. All would be "right." Clearly, the senses are of considerable value, provided you regard them as your servants and not your masters. Greater tolerance to changes in climate can be of great value. For instance, if you feel cold, then you let your circulation slow down and

begin to feel even colder, which increases your mental agitation. This situation can be eased, both mentally and physically by the exercises shown here.

The position below provides a body lock and gives a strong stimulus. Hold it for about five minutes and you will begin to sweat, whatever the weather.

1 *Sit up on your heels, making fists of the hands and placing them on the knees, with the elbows well tucked in.*

2 *Breathe in and, retaining the breath, bend forward slowly until your forehead touches the fists. Do not let the elbows slip out. The breathing will be constricted, but keep it quite slow. Hold for several minutes, or as long as you are not too uncomfortable, then slowly straighten up, breathing in.*

INCREASING CIRCULATION

1 Another powerful way to combat the cold is to stand comfortably erect. Having breathed out, close the left nostril with the third finger of the right hand and breathe in deeply through the right nostril. Then again bring the right arm down by the side.

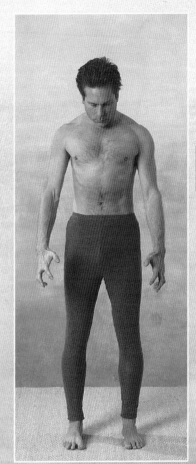

1

2 Retaining the breath, tense every muscle of the body, from the top of the head to the tip of the toe. Do this until the whole body begins to shake. Then breathe out slowly through both nostrils and relax. This will have stimulated the flow of blood through the whole body.

> **CAUTION** This technique and that on the facing page should not be attempted by those suffering from heart conditions, hypertension, or chest problems. If in any doubt, consult a specialist or your physician.

THE POWER OF THE MIND

While the two techniques shown are highly effective if carried out correctly, there is no doubt that the finest way of opposing sensory impressions is by using the mind. Controlled experiments have shown that body temperatures can actually be raised – or lowered – by the process of visualization. On one occasion in Britain, a man sat in a room with the temperature at 35°F, with a woollen shawl, steeped in freezing water, around his bare trunk. He sat and visualized a hot beach in Italy where he had been on vacation, imagining himself swimming in the sea and then lying in the sun without drying his skin. The shawl dried completely in 105 minutes and during this time he maintained his body temperature. He suffered no ill effects.

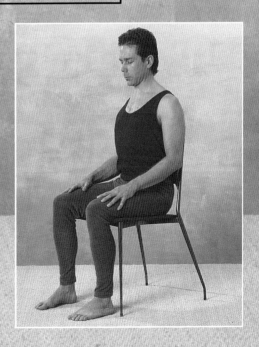

FACING THE CHALLENGES

COOLING DOWN

Specific techniques that have been developed over the years will give you an important degree of control over your senses and will also help you to understand that control and beneficial moderation play an important role in your life.

In the same way that there are physically based methods for making yourself feel warmer, so you can use a similar approach to cool yourself down. The basis of the technique is the ability to curl the tongue. This is best tried initially while looking into a mirror.

SIPPING THE AIR

By curling the tongue the air is drawn straight into the body and, at
the same time, you concentrate on an impression of coolness – sucking
an ice cream, for example!

1

1 Sitting correctly, on the floor or in a chair, breathe
out, open the mouth, and let the curled tongue peep
through. Then inhale, drawing the air in through a series of
short sips, not in a continuous flow.

2 Next, close the mouth, retain the air for a few
seconds, and then breathe slowly out through the
nostrils. This should be repeated a number of times, sensing
that however hot it is, the air still strikes a little cool on the
tongue as you breathe in.

It is not simply a matter of learning these techniques by rote, but of
examining challenges as they arise and, using the principles you have
learned, to devise your own methods of facing them. Life is a process
of self-realization and everyone has an individual part to play.

A SEDENTARY LIFESTYLE

THE HA BREATH

*For millions of people, especially in the Western world, life has become
increasingly sedentary in recent years. This brings with it a number of
new health hazards. One important aspect of this is that such lack of activity
affects the breath.*

The absence of regular challenging physical movement not only fails
to provide an adequate stimulus to the heart and the circulation, it
also results in stale air lying in the lungs, since the shallow breathing
that accompanies this lifestyle prevents the lungs from being used
properly. The exercise shown below, called the Ha Breath, ensures that
the lungs are filled with fresh air.

1 *In a standing position,
having breathed out, breathe
in deeply through the nose, bending
the knees slightly and swinging the
arms back over the head.*

2 As you breathe out, letting the arms
swing down in front of you, open the
mouth and let the air flow out, emitting a
strong "Ha" sound. Tense the abdominal
muscles to push the diaphragm up farther. Let
the arms dangle and hold the position for
some seconds before repeating. Three or four
full breaths carried out in this manner will
ensure that the lungs are filled with fresh air.

MAKING THE LUNGS WORK

The Ha Breath and the technique below are very effective, but if your lifestyle is not active, it is also sensible to break off from time to time during the day to ensure that full effective breathing is taking place and that the bottom ribs are activating diaphragmatic movement. With so many people now working on word processors, computers and other desk-bound tasks, new environmental health hazards are developing, such as repetitive strain injury. An integral part of such problems will be ineffectual breathing. Correcting this, together with effective postural exercises, will bring immense relief to cramped muscles.

1

1 An alternative manner of refreshing the lungs is to sit on the knees, linking the fingers behind the back. Swing up on an in-breath, stretching the arms away from the back.

2 Now, breathing out through the mouth in a series of puffs, bring the trunk down and stretch the arms right up into the air. On the downward bend, aim to bring the forehead to the ground, with the arms at a right-angle from the trunk. Hold the air out for a few seconds and repeat two or three times.

POSITIVE THOUGHTS

SHARE YOUR BLESSINGS

Countless books have been produced telling us to enhance our lives by thinking positive thoughts. The late Emil Cue suggested that everyone should say to themselves: "Every day and in every way, I feel better and better." If that had really worked, we should all be doing it by now! The true positive path is to accept that there are problems to be countered while understanding that you have the capacity to counter them through the life breath.

The need to think positively is undeniable, but the most positive thing about life is the breath. If we are embracing life, the breath is full and liberated. If we are frightened or angry, it is constricted and shallow. Mankind has succeeded in grabbing both land and water for personal profit, but so far has been unable to turn the air into a negotiable commodity. We all share the breath of life. We all draw in life with every breath. We all distribute it again each time we breathe out. Taking and sharing – the basis of life itself – need to be equal. A grabbing attitude to life results in disaster; unbalanced giving is equally harmful. Let the breath teach us the balance of living.

IN	OUT
I draw in the force of life with my breath.	I share life every time I exhale.
Life is a wonderful experience.	I must share this experience with others.
As I draw the breath in, I am strong.	But realizing the needs of others does not diminish my strength.
My breath and my consciousness are one.	Both breath and consciousness are universal.
Breath and consciousness are eternal.	I am free from fear.

1

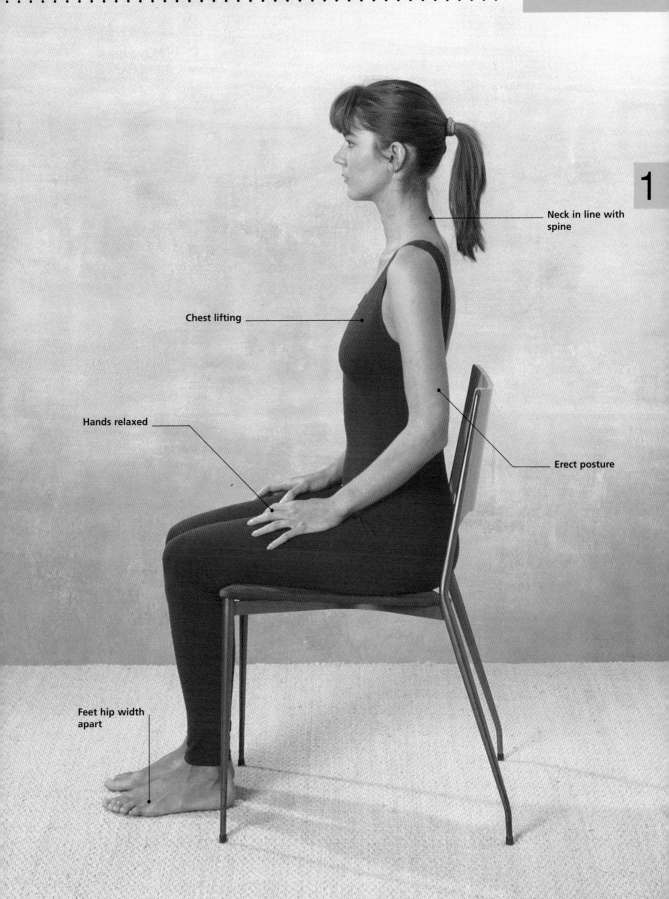

Neck in line with
spine

Chest lifting

Erect posture

Hands relaxed

Feet hip width
apart

NATURAL THERAPIES

Self-awareness provides humans with two remarkable, natural therapies: sobbing and laughter. Each of these uses the same principle – a very strong pumping motion to force out blockages of energy, both mental and physical.

SOBBING

If you have a blocked drain, then you use a rubber plunger to free it by creating a repeated vacuum. In the same way the human plunger overcomes the stagnation of depression and the inflammation of fear. Bottling up emotion can be very harmful. Westerners, especially, tend to be urged not to show their feelings – "stiff upper lip!" – no matter what damage is being done under the surface. If something unhappy, unsettling or frightening happens, a short sharp bout of sobbing can have a most beneficial effect. The physical rationale is precisely the same here as in hearty laughter. The sob expels the air sharply, letting it flow in once more. This stimulates the pumping of the diaphragm and the seized-up body begins to function normally again. It is not, of course, a good idea to make sobbing a way of life! But as a way of releasing pent-up feelings it can be highly therapeutic.

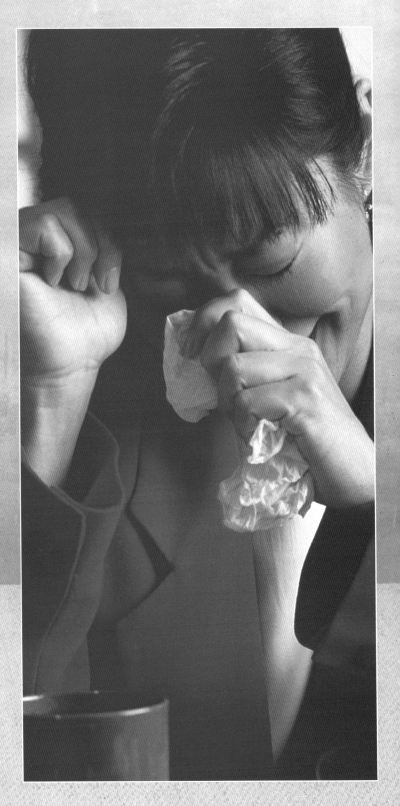

LAUGHTER

Norman Cousins, former editor of *The Saturday Review*, overcame a disabling illness that confined him to a wheelchair by taking large doses of Vitamin C and constantly screening comedy films that made him laugh. Now American doctors are realizing the therapeutic value of laughter and are bringing fun into hospitals.

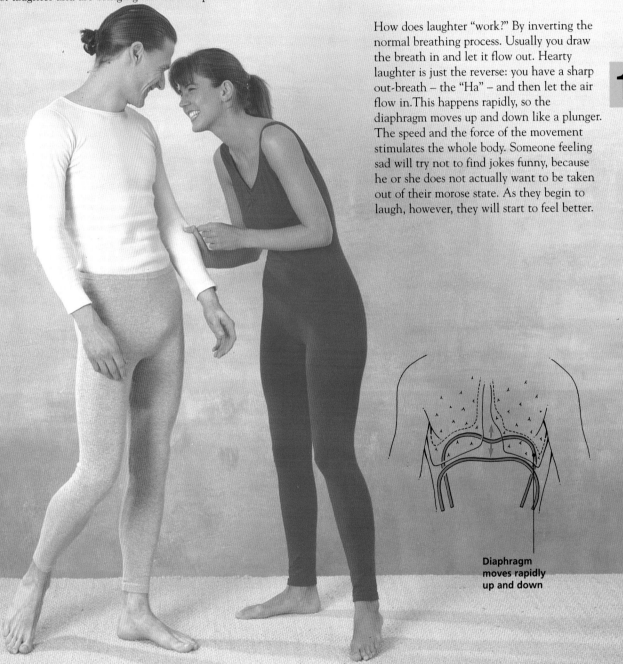

**Diaphragm
moves rapidly
up and down**

How does laughter "work?" By inverting the normal breathing process. Usually you draw the breath in and let it flow out. Hearty laughter is just the reverse: you have a sharp out-breath – the "Ha" – and then let the air flow in. This happens rapidly, so the diaphragm moves up and down like a plunger. The speed and the force of the movement stimulates the whole body. Someone feeling sad will try not to find jokes funny, because he or she does not actually want to be taken out of their morose state. As they begin to laugh, however, they will start to feel better.

1

In addition to Cousins's method – reading humorous books, watching funny movies and television programs – you can also stimulate yourself. Stand with the hands on the hips, the feet apart, start to shout out, "Hi!" as loudly as you can and swing the trunk about as you do it. This will have a strong effect on the diaphragm and you will be forcing energy round the body. Probably you will not want to do this in front of other people – to start with anyhow – so choose somewhere where you will not be seen or heard.

ANALYZING YOUR HEALTH

It is important that this book should be read as a whole. Ideas are given to assist in combatting a variety of different chronic conditions, but if these are looked at in isolation obviously they will be inadequate. By studying the whole

Condition	18-19	20-21	22-23	24-25	26-27	28-29	30-31	32-33	34-35	36-37	38-39	40-41	42-43	44-45	46-47	48-49	50-51	52-53	54-55	56-57	58-59
Allergies																					
Headaches																					
High blood pressure																					
Asthma																					
Tension						●															
Arthritis																					
Severe fatigue													●								
Jet lag																					
Common cold																					
Eyestrain																					
Insomnia						●							●								
Spine strengthening							●														
Stiffness							●														
Cancer																					
Circulation							●							●		●					
Diabetes																					
Epilepsy																					
Emotion control																					
Energy boost										●			●							●	
Heart																					●
Feeling cold														●							
Feeling hot															●						
Clearing lungs																●					
Depression											●							●			
Pollution																●					
Stress											●	●									

Use this handy cross-reference chart to pinpoint the pages that contain information on a number of commonly suffered problems and conditions.

book, it is possible to make considerable day-by-day changes that will enhance life
and play an important role in opposing difficulties. This is not a book of "cures,"
but one of maximizing your capacity to achieve a better and healthier life.

Page 60-61
Page 62-63
Page 64-65
Page 66-67
Page 68-69
Page 70-71
Page 72-73
Page 74-75
Page 76-77
Page 78-79
Page 80-81
Page 82-83
Page 84-85
Page 86-87
Page 88-89
Page 90-91
Page 92-93
Page 94
Page 95
Page 96
Page 97
Page 98-99
Page 100-101
Page 102-103
Page 104-105
Page 106-107
Page 108-109
Page 110-111
Page 112-113
Page 114-115
Page 116-117
Page 118-119
Page 120-121
Page 122-123

2

THE PHILOSOPHY OF RESPIRATION

MAINTAINING THE LIFE FORCE

Because, as has already been stressed, breath is life, there is no aspect of existence in which it does not play a direct and central role: every thought depends upon electrical signals between the neurons and a multi-oxygenated brain; every movement, every stretch depends upon the same forces — electro-magnetism and oxygenation.

Some, though by no means all, medical professionals have been dismissive about the idea of paying special attention to breathing. One commented contemptuously: "Birds and animals don't even know they are breathing and they get along alright." True, but it is the very fact that humans *do* know that makes all the difference.

This is not the place to theorize about how human consciousness has developed: the important point is that it has and that it is the dominant factor of human lives. An Indian swami remarked sagely: "The cause of death … is birth." Similarly, the effective maintenance of life depends upon the effective maintenance of the life force – breath.

In general terms, you probably know that stretching is good for you. Often you will do impromptu stretches after waking up or after feeling cramped and confined. At such times you will find, too, that you breathe deeply with the movement, to stretch the lungs and to send an invigorating flow of energy through the body. By paying attention to the breath and the central role it plays, you are taking this natural and healthy instinct and developing it for the benefit of a happier, fitter life.

2

If you are out in the country, or by the sea, on a lovely sunny day and look at the beauty of nature, you may have a glowing feeling of oneness. "I feel a part of it," you might say and automatically you will have enhanced your breathing to match the feeling. Are there any limitations to the benefits that better breathing can bring? Nobody knows. What is known is that every aspect of life is changing continually and the central factor is *how* that change comes about. What is incontrovertible is that the combination of mind and breath is the most powerful combined weapon you have. Used negatively, it can not only damage but also destroy; used positively, it can bring about amazing changes for the better. Following the quest along this path is a tremendous adventure.

APPROACH TO LIFE

TYPE A PERSON

Medical research in the 1970s found that what was described as the Type A person, tense and working to deadlines, produced a high susceptibility to heart disease.

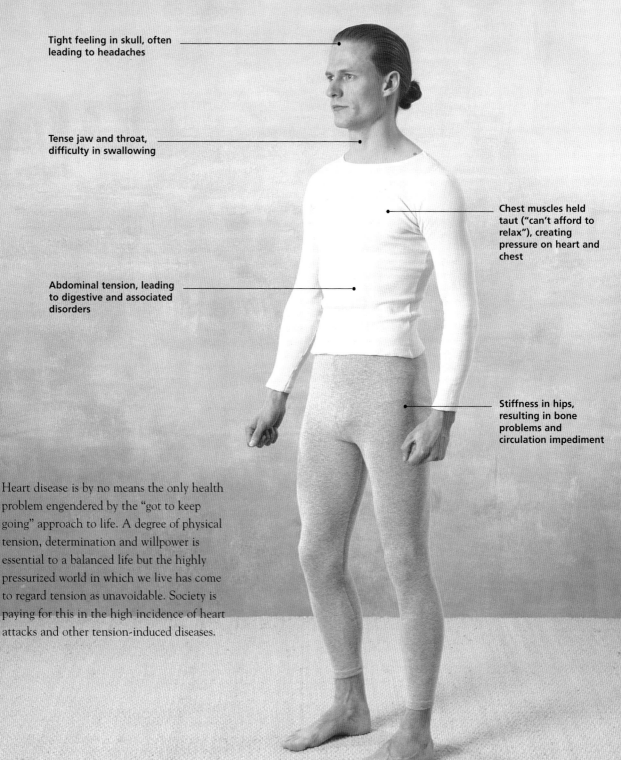

Tight feeling in skull, often leading to headaches

Tense jaw and throat, difficulty in swallowing

Chest muscles held taut ("can't afford to relax"), creating pressure on heart and chest

Abdominal tension, leading to digestive and associated disorders

Stiffness in hips, resulting in bone problems and circulation impediment

Heart disease is by no means the only health problem engendered by the "got to keep going" approach to life. A degree of physical tension, determination and willpower is essential to a balanced life but the highly pressurized world in which we live has come to regard tension as unavoidable. Society is paying for this in the high incidence of heart attacks and other tension-induced diseases.

TYPE B PERSON

*At the same time it was claimed that the Type B person had a more placid outlook
and thus suffered fewer heart problems. All too often, however, they feel
swamped by life's problems.*

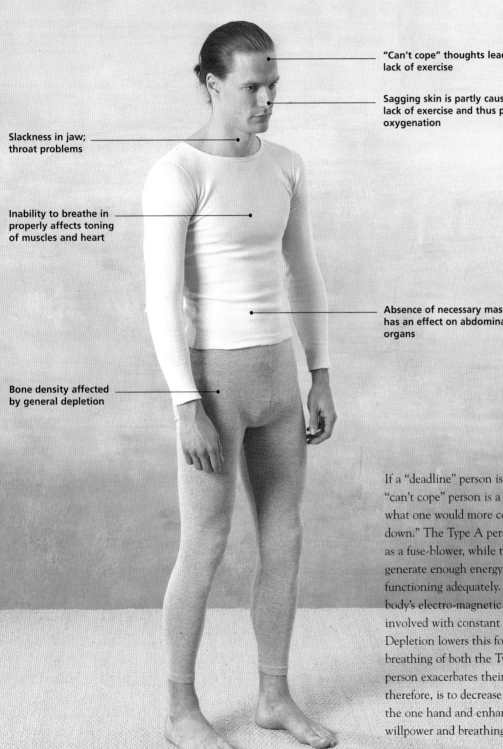

"Can't cope" thoughts lead to
lack of exercise

Sagging skin is partly caused by
lack of exercise and thus poor
oxygenation

Slackness in jaw;
throat problems

Inability to breathe in
properly affects toning
of muscles and heart

Absence of necessary massage
has an effect on abdominal
organs

Bone density affected
by general depletion

2

If a "deadline" person is a bundle of stress, a
"can't cope" person is a bundle of depletion or
what one would more commonly call "run
down." The Type A person can be looked on
as a fuse-blower, while the Type B one fails to
generate enough energy to keep the systems
functioning adequately. For instance, the
body's electro-magnetic force is centrally
involved with constant bone replacement.
Depletion lowers this force. The shallow
breathing of both the Type A and Type B
person exacerbates their problems. Your aim,
therefore, is to decrease tension and strain on
the one hand and enhance effective
willpower and breathing on the other.

BALANCING RELAXATION
AND ENERGIZATION

PROMOTING FITNESS

Although there are all sorts of exercise programs to promote and maintain fitness, some principles are all too often overlooked. One is to link the breath effectively with the activity; another is to balance tension and relaxation – again as much in breathing as in body movement.

Homo sapiens is the only species to have developed a naturally upright stance and walk as their only form of locomotion. The process of walking is a difficult balance, since for most of the time humans have only one leg on the ground. To assist balance we have developed quadrilateralism – swinging the opposite arm to the leg being lifted.

1 March, either on the spot or around the room, swinging the opposite arm to the leg being lifted, with a corresponding rapid – but not shallow – breath. This stimulates the heartbeat and circulation.

2 Lie on your back and bicycle with your legs to the rhythm of the breath. This improves leg circulation.

3 *Trunk, heart and arms are benefited by swinging the arms up freely to the in-breath and letting them fall to the out-breath.*

2

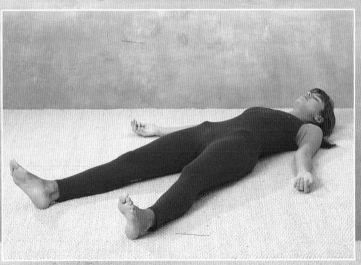

4 These invigorating actions should be followed by total relaxation, as already shown (pages 24–5). If you are tense or agitated, it is useless to attempt to relax, but if the heart is pumping quite strongly and the blood flowing freely – if you are a little "puffed" – the body's need to calm down will take over and relaxation can then be effective, giving you the best of both worlds.

LETTING ENERGY FLOW

RESTORING FLEXIBILITY

*Humans have a wonderful self-help kit: a pair of flexible hands. In developing
your breathing to enhance your health, the self-help aspect plays an
important role.*

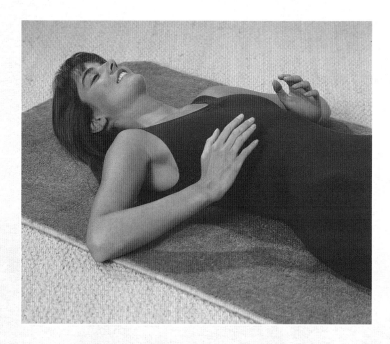

It must be remembered that ribs are
comparatively flexible bones, designed to
move and impelled by the attached muscles.
Often, through mental and physical tensions,
breathing becomes so affected that this
muscle flexibility is lost and the ribs fail to
perform an essential part of their function. By
responding to the pressure of your own hands,
you can help to restore this flexibility and
improve the quality of the breath.

*1 Lying on the back, place the hands on the
side (not the top) of the rib cage, so the
pads of the hands are covering the bottom two
ribs. As you breathe in, let the hands become
quite limp and relaxed.*

*2 On the out-breath, press the hands firmly
against the ribs, squeezing them toward
the center. Hold for two or three seconds after
the breath is out and then breathe in again,
with no pressure from the hands. This
squeezing movement will deepen the out-breath
and encourage the ribs to spring out on the
enhanced in-breath. If you feel a tendency to
breathe too fast, this can be gradually corrected
by maintaining the pressure with your hands
for a second or two longer.*

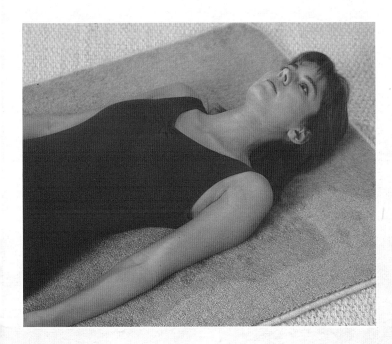

3 Having "worked" the ribs for two or three minutes – a dozen or so breaths – remove the hands, continuing to breathe in the same way and be aware of the enhanced depth and efficiency you are achieving. On the in-breath, feel the sense of physical pressure from the muscle contraction and the flow of air into the lungs.

2

4 As you breathe out, feel the sensation of release. The muscles relax, the air flows through the nostrils, and the diaphragm moves up. By practicing this exercise regularly, the improvement in your normal breath will become automatic with resulting benefit from day to day.

CAUTION It must be remembered that anyone who has cracked a rib recently, or who has osteoporosis, should not attempt this and should merely visualize the movement.

BETTER BREATHING

IMPROVING MUSCLE TONE

Every aspect of body functioning is intended to operate on its own rhythm, each in harmony with the rhythm of breath and heartbeat. As tensions of all sorts reflect themselves in the breath, so the other body rhythms are impeded and, in due course, these become symptoms of ill-health.

As you enhance the effectiveness of your breathing, so you can also detect problems that have arisen and, in many cases, soothe them away.

After lying down and developing an efficient natural breath, as described on the preceding pages, place the hands gently on the chest.

Feel the beneficial tension that arises as the muscles contract, the air flows in and the lungs expand. Then, as you breathe out, be aware of and encourage the muscle relaxation and feel the slow passage of air through the nostrils. This helps to ensure the efficiency of the chest muscles and the effectiveness of the heart massage.

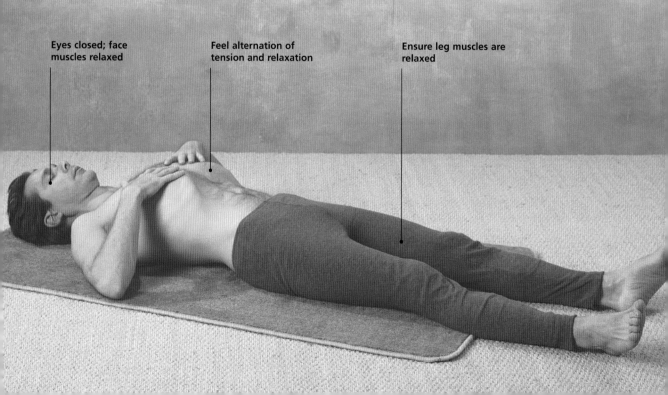

Eyes closed; face muscles relaxed

Feel alternation of tension and relaxation

Ensure leg muscles are relaxed

DETECTING ABDOMINAL TENSION

One aspect of the respiration process is to promote the functioning of the abdominal organs. Bad posture and emotional tensions can have a highly damaging effect. A gentle, personal massage is an important part of the process of health.

Having checked the chest movement for several breaths, you should now transfer the hands to the abdomen. Do nothing as you breathe in, but use your fingertips to massage slowly from just below the ribcage as you breathe out. The whole area should feel relaxed, but you may detect pockets of tension, especially in the area of the colon. If the breathing is truly balanced, the feeling of relaxation should cover the whole of the abdomen. Massage evenly and work on any areas that are tight or lumpy. Remember, the abdomen needs to be tense on the in-breath, but should relax wholly on the out-breath.

CAUTION Do not jab or poke at sore or painful areas. If they do not respond after some days of practice, consult your physician; it could save a great deal of suffering in the future.

2

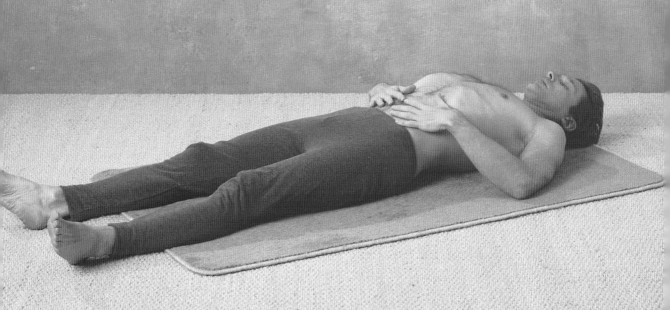

BRAIN MESSAGES

THE EFFECTS OF SUPPRESSED ANGER

Many people confuse "acceptance" and "putting up with." If you feel you have to put up with a situation, the mental reluctance results in a whole series of inhibitory messages going out from the brain and central to these messages is restricted breathing.

This breathing mirrors the irked, sometimes downright angry, mental state and helps to convey the emotion through the body. Muscles contract as an expression of the unwillingness to accept and aspects of the body's "transportation system" – blood circulation and the transmission of bioenergetic substances hormones, antibodies and so on – will be impaired. So you then blame circumstances for making you feel tense and unwell. You may know this is illogical; there is nothing you can do immediately about the situation, but in a perverse way it can be satisfactory to feel unhappy and below par. Most meditative spiritual teachings urge calmness and acceptance of a situation through sitting upright, closing the eyes, and seeking to compose yourself. This is effective, but it is interesting that the lesser-known teaching of the Jains, a religion with total respect for all forms of life, includes a standing position of acceptance.

Feel you are breathing from the heart

Fingers are wholly relaxed

Stand comfortably upright, with the arms just a little distance away from the thighs. This is linked to calm, controlled, slow breathing. In today's busy world the Jains' approach can often be more practical than sitting with closed eyes. The combination of simple, upright posture and calm breathing can take you from resentment to acceptance.

THE JAINS' APPROACH

Acceptance, in the sense used in this book, does not mean that no action can be taken to improve the situation – rather that the right course is more likely to become apparent through calmness of mind and body, than through resentment and tensing up.

When a calmer understanding develops of how to deal with the present situation, you can move from acceptance to affirmation. When you are resenting a circumstance and putting up with it reluctantly, you tend to go in on yourself. The tension produces an uneasy mix of withdrawal and aggression – the "don't you dare touch me ... I'm the wronged party" attitude. After the edge of this emotional state has been taken off by combining a controlled, slow breath with a simple physical posture, you can move a little farther toward a more positive attitude.

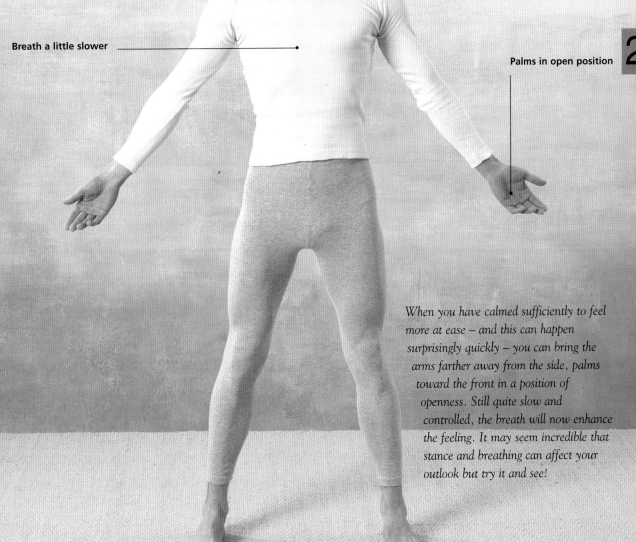

Breath a little slower

Palms in open position

2

When you have calmed sufficiently to feel more at ease – and this can happen surprisingly quickly – you can bring the arms farther away from the side, palms toward the front in a position of openness. Still quite slow and controlled, the breath will now enhance the feeling. It may seem incredible that stance and breathing can affect your outlook but try it and see!

AIRBORNE POLLUTION

THE NOSE AS A FILTER

It is undeniable that much of the planet is polluted and a great deal of the pollution is carried on the air. Much, though not all of this, is human-created.

As a result, investigations into many forms of illness are concentrated on the dangers of pollution: exhaust fumes, cigarette smoke, pesticides and so on. There can be little doubt these factors do have a significant effect, though much more often as triggers than actual causes. Cleaning up the air is therefore important, but both attitude of mind and correct, natural breathing are equally so in maintaining health.

First, you need to understand that nature has long recognized the dangers of pollution and has taken its own steps to minimize the effects. While there are two basic methods of taking in the breath of life, the mouth is an emergency system, designed only to be used on certain specific occasions. The nostrils are the central breathing apparatus and include two essential functions: to warm the air as it passes into the body and to remove as much dirt and pollution as possible. Constant breathing through the mouth will, of course, negate this important precaution and anxiety about the dangers of pollution will also impair the breathing process, making nature's measures ineffectual.

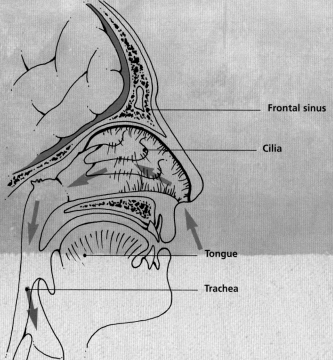

Frontal sinus

Cilia

Tongue

Trachea

The tiny hairs in the nostrils, called the cilia, trap many of the unwanted particles, preventing them from going into the lungs. By cleaning the nose, in Western society by the use of a handkerchief or tissue, aided by the mucus which lubricates the organ, the trapped particles are taken away and the cilia continue their function.

COPING WITH POLLUTION

Clearly, we should all resolve to make whatever contribution we can to achieving a cleaner atmosphere. However, in the meantime, you can work on affirming your capacity to counter the difficulties, naturally and calmly. Fear and agitation promote the very effect that you would like to avoid – shallow breathing, pollution remaining in lungs rather than being expelled, increased asthma risk and abdominal tension.

2

Remember that deep breathing is not necessary: what is important is that the air inhaled does its rightful job, flowing through the lungs and stimulating all aspects of body energy. This can be achieved by moderate, slow, rhythmical breathing, with the diaphragm functioning effectively. In this way you minimize the dangers round you, though you cannot eliminate them. In addition, while in an obviously polluted area, it is important to have a good supply of handkerchiefs or tissues, as the cilia will quickly get overloaded. Remember always to clear one nostril at a time. On reaching a relatively less polluted atmosphere, practicing the exercises for changing the air in the lungs (see pages 48–9 and 77) will be invaluable.

Most people, either regularly or occasionally, will have to be in major cities and areas where pollution can be rife. Even in beautiful-looking countryside the air may be polluted.

ALLERGIC REACTIONS

ROLE OF STRESS

Allergies have many causes. Some are deep-seated and may never be eradicated, but only alleviated. Others are triggered or exacerbated by stress. In all cases, massage and effective breathing will ease abdominal tension, which plays a major role in the building up of food allergies, and can calm agitated feelings.

Some people are allergic to specific foods, such as dairy products or the gluten in cereal grains.

The brilliant interlinked design of the human body relates the flow of energy, in its myriad forms, with the necessary rhythmical massage of the glands and organs of the abdomen. Living and breathing harmoniously, the diaphragm moves up and down, alternately slightly squeezing and then releasing the abdominal area. In this way a gentle flushing of blood keeps the organs functioning well and the hardening process, in part induced by ineffectual and inharmonious breathing, is opposed naturally.

RESPONSE TO TOUCH

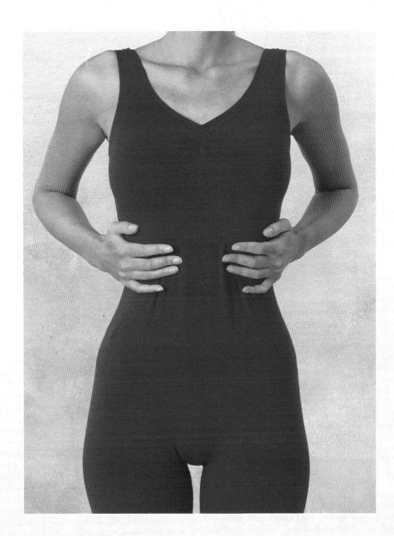

2

Lie down in the relaxation position described on pages 24–5, allow a minute or two of quiet, automatic breathing, with the abdomen gently rising and falling, then begin to breathe a little more deeply, with the bottom ribs taking over the motion. When this has assumed a rhythmical pattern, place the fingertips just below the ribs and each time you breathe out, gently massage the abdominal area – but *only* on the out-breath.

It is not necessary to know anything about the art of massage itself. The fingers are just exploring whether the sense of relaxation is complete. Certain areas may feel tense or lumpy; if so, pay them more – though always gentle – attention. Your body responds to the touch of your own fingers and areas that have seized up will tend to relax as a result of the massage. Familiarity with your body will help you to prevent health problems.

> **CAUTION If the allergy persists despite effective breathing and accompanying massage you will need to consult a physician or therapist. This is also the case if you discover persistant hardness or pain in the abdomen.**

HEADACHES

COMBINING FINGERS AND BREATHING

As you perceive pain, you automatically tend to seize up against it. The tension caused by the pain is then intensified and this enhances and perpetuates the severe discomfort.

A headache is a common form of pain and this causes a mental reaction, as a result of which the brain sends out a whole series of inhibitory messages. Often a headache will lift when something happens to divert your attention away from it. As you cannot rely on this, you need to be able to take matters – literally – into your own hands. Pain constricts the breathing, but, though it takes an effort of will, you can open up the breath and feel it flowing more and more calmly. Combine this breathing with the soothing effects of your own fingers to smooth headaches away.

1 Place the fingers, just touching, on the forehead. As you breathe in let them move apart lightly.

2 Then, as you breathe out, move them together again. Just concentrate on the pleasure of the touch and a sensation of peace. Often even a stubborn headache will respond quite quickly.

THE BACK OF THE HEAD

Many headaches occur specifically at the back of the head, tensing up the muscles in the area. Massage can make a considerable difference, but it is also helpful to loosen the taut muscles as shown here.

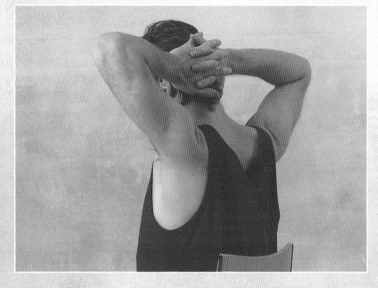

1 First, link the fingers together on the back of the neck, parallel with the ears.

2 Having breathed in, as you breathe out, firmly – but not jerkily – begin to bring the head down. Continue until the chin touches the chest – or as nearly so as possible.

2

3 Hold the position, with the breath out, for several seconds and then slowly straighten up, breathing in. Repeat – within reason – as often as seems necessary.

HIGH BLOOD PRESSURE

RELAXATION METHODS

In the 1970s the British Medical Journal revealed that no less than one-third of the Western adult population suffers from hypertension – high blood-pressure. Many factors are involved, but there can be no doubt that the highly pressurized society we have created plays a prominent role.

An Indian medical practitioner, Dr. Chandra Patel, conducted two significant trials about 20 years ago into the ability of yoga relaxation to normalize blood pressure in groups of subjects, some of whom had been taking medication for a number of years. The results were quite remarkable. Dr. Patel used the relaxation method, lying on the ground (see pages 24–5). Undoubtedly this can be immensely effective. In our rushed lives, however, we need also to be able to make use of quite brief moments to check the symptoms. Calm breathing and the art of visualization can be brought together to be fitted into the day at almost any time.

Sitting comfortably upright in a chair, preferably with the eyes closed, the breath is brought quietly under control. The quiet, rhythmical sound of the breath reminds you of the waves on the seashore and, as you let the out-breath become longer than the in-breath, you can imagine the tide is ebbing. In your mind's eye, in coordination with the breath, you see the waves rolling in and then, as you breathe out, the water receding. Slowly, but surely, the tide is going out. A feeling of peace comes over you.

LOSING BAD HABITS

Most people accumulate a lot of little habits in their lives that tend to push up their blood pressure. One is getting too bogged down by time – the "I've gotta fit it all in" approach.

Become aware of other habits that create moments of tension. Answering the telephone might be one. Let it ring a couple more times while you control your breath before answering. When this approach has become clear, you will find a number of other small ways to reinforce the message of calming down.

2

One way of freeing yourself from the time trap is to stick a small colored circle on your wrist watch, so that every time you look at it you are reminded to take a few quiet breaths and slow down.

CHEST PROBLEMS

CONTROLLING PANIC ATTACKS

In the West, chest complaints and asthma are reaching epidemic proportions.
Moderate symptoms are disturbing, but a severe asthmatic attack can be fatal.
Any form of breathlessness or chest seizure is alarming and the resulting fear then
intensifies the breathing problem.

1 One helpful way of countering this fear is
deliberately to open up the chest. Sit on
the heels, linking the hands behind the back.
Breathing in, swing back, stretching the hands
away from the back.

2 On the out-breath begin to swing
downward, raising the arms as high as
possible. Make the movement slow, but
maintain the swinging impetus, rather like the
pendulum of a stately grandfather clock. Let
both movement and breathing capacity develop
slowly. Do not get impatient.

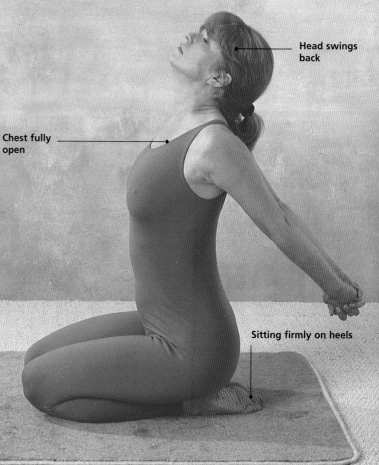

Head swings
back

Chest fully
open

Sitting firmly on heels

CLEARING THE LUNGS

Pollution and shallow breathing cause a build-up of mucous and harmful substances in the lungs. The exercise below will help to clear the lungs, but read the caution before you try. Three or four of these movements can also help to reduce the severity of asthmatic attack.

Head erect

Elbows well back

Feet a few inches apart

2

1   *Stand, feet a little apart, arms by the side. After an out-breath, breathe in, slowly bringing the arms out to the side. When they are parallel with the shoulders, bend them and place the fingertips on the shoulders.*

2   *Retaining the breath, drop the head, bring the elbows to the front and squeeze the chest, exerting a controlled pressure on the lungs. Hold for a few seconds, then, breathing out, raise the head, bring the elbows out and lower the arms to the side.*

CAUTION If the condition is severe, or if emphysema has resulted, great caution is necessary and specialist medical advice should be sought.

LACK OF SLEEP

IMPORTANCE OF IMAGERY

A high proportion of people suffer from insomnia from time to time in their lives. In many people it is a persistent problem. Certain factors need to be stressed: the importance of winding-down before going to bed (see pages 27 and 43), and not indulging in heavy drinking or eating late at night.

Imagery is an important factor. Whether this technique is used before going to bed, or when sitting up in bed, creating a visualization of calmness can be valuable. Here is just one idea:

1 Bring the hands together in front of the chest, with fingers and thumbs touching. Breathe out.

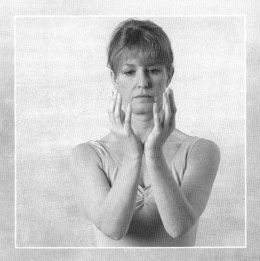

2 As you breathe in, let the fingers and thumbs open out, like the petals of a lotus or water lily.

3 At the same time bring into your mind the calm beauty of this lovely plant, with the sun glinting on the still waters of a lake. Breathe slowly, imagining this wholly peaceful scene. Finish on an out-breath, closing the petals for the night and settle down to sleep.

FEELING DROWSY

*As you begin to move toward sleep, the initial relaxation leads to gentle abdominal
breathing, which in turn promotes a sense of drowsiness. As sleep takes over, so
the breath moves up into the thorax. You cannot hope to sleep if – deliberately or
inadvertently – you are breathing in a non-sleep manner.*

Bear in mind the pattern of how you move to
sleep-breathing, and stand, sit, or lie on the
back in bed. Ensure the conscious breath is
free by steadily encouraging the bottom ribs
to move (as shown on page 62). Remember
the breath does not need to be deep, but the
movement must become easy. When this has
been achieved, remove the hands to the side
and let the breath become relaxed and
automatic. The abdomen will begin gently to
move. Having accustomed yourself to letting
the breath be free, this will bring about a
feeling of drowsiness. Your awareness will
have dimmed, but you can still feel the
breathing moving up into the chest – before
you nod off!

2

JET LAG

RESTORING INTERNAL RHYTHMS

Human bodies function on what is called the Circadian Rhythm – approximately a 24-hour cycle – with many internal rhythms harmonizing with this pattern. Jet lag and working a variety of different shifts both interfere with these rhythms, throwing the body and brain out of harmony.

On long flights it is important to make sure your clothes are as loose as possible. You will feel more comfortable if you remove your shoes, but because your feet tend to swell, try to wear shoes that will slip on easily. From time to time on the journey, close your eyes and breathe slowly, paying special attention to the out-breath. This will ease tensions within the brain and body and encourage the circulation flow. Shift workers should follow the same breathing pattern, wherever possible. Two or three minutes at a time are quite sufficient.

Response to jet lag and varied shifts differs from person to person, but acceptance plays a major role. Apprehension or other negative emotions will create tension in mind and body, often with damaging effects.

After a flight of several hours, or at the end of an awkward working shift, it is immensely beneficial to spend some time in the lying pose of relaxation. Following the principles on pages 24–5, choose a draft-free carpeted floor and let yourself completely relax for at least 10 minutes. Allow the breath to be quiet and natural. Say to yourself, "I am not breathing; my body is breathing." As you feel the tension disappear, become aware of the rise and fall of the abdomen. It may help to say "peace" to yourself with each out-breath.

2

THE HEART

. . . .

CARDIOGRAPHIC TRACES

*The heart is the most powerful force of electrical generation in the body. Its beat is
linked to the state of brain and mind via the respiration. Electrocardiograms are
now used routinely to monitor the functioning of the heart, so you can see clearly
how the electrical impulses are responding.*

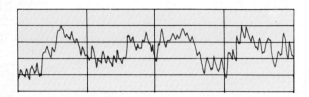

Just how dramatic the changes can be is
demonstrated by the two cardiographic traces
shown. In the one above, frustration and
resentment, which often do not produce a
strong external appearance, are resulting in

harsh and harmful changes within the heart.
In the instance below, the emotions expressed
are happiness and acceptance and the
beneficial rhythmic flow of the heartbeat is
clear to see.

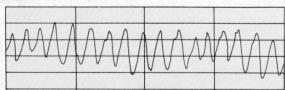

Changes can take place very fast, due to
change of mood, with a resultant alteration in
the breathing patterns. This will apply both
to emotional responses and to the way you
react to pain and other symptoms of physical
malfunction. Obviously, the more the heart is

subjected to violent swings such as these, or
to the pressures of unrelieved tension, the
more it is put at risk. Remember, heart
conditions are still the single largest cause of
death in Western countries.

RELEASING TENSIONS

*One way of dealing with harmful tensions is to accept them and then to release
them. It may be helpful, if anti-social, to smash all the crockery in overcoming
your rage; it is far better if you can reduce tension in a controlled way.*

*1 First of all accept the tension, feeling it seize up body
and breath – even accentuate it by clenching the fists
until they hurt. You will find that the breath has been
roughly retained.*

2

*2 Now, open the hands sharply, spreading the fingers,
and breathe out strongly. Repeat this several times:
each time you do so, the sense of release from the tension
will grow and the feeling of relaxation with the out-breath
will become greater. You have taken a valuable step in
normalizing breathing and heartbeat.*

VULNERABLE JOINTS

FROZEN SHOULDER

*Joints can seize up for a variety of reasons, but when this has happened,
psychological difficulties can play a major role in slowing or preventing natural
repair. The brain can associate an emotional upset with physical pain, resulting in
additional tension in the affected area. The discomfort often has an effect on
breathing, making matters worse.*

"Frozen shoulder" is a somewhat omnibus
term for what can be an irksome, painful
disability. Working consciously to restore a
free breathing pattern will diminish the
seizing-up effect resulting from the damage
and the healing process will be enhanced.

1 *Sit comfortably in a chair,
hands on the lap and spend three
or four minutes breathing effectively,
feeling the bottom ribs move up and out on
the inhalation, down on the out-breath,
with the abdomen still. When this has
become rhythmical, raise the affected arm
slowly on the in-breath, visualizing energy
flowing into the shoulder. You will be
surprised to find that it moves more than
you expected, with little or no pain. Do not
rush anything and be content to make
slow progress*

2 *From time to time
balance the action by
using both arms. So long as
there is discomfort and some
immobility in the shoulder,
continue to visualize the glow
of warm energy there with
every in-breath.*

TENNIS ELBOW

"Tennis elbow" – sometimes called "golfer's elbow" – can be helped similarly. Again, from a comfortable sitting position, promote an effective energizing breath until the breath is functioning rhythmically. It will then be reducing the damage in the joint.

1 Stretch the affected arm in front of you, visualize the glow of energy at the point of the elbow and bend the arm gently on the in-breath, straightening it again as you breathe out. Always remember: slow but sure.

2 As with the shoulder, also work both arms, bringing them up as you breathe in. Hold as you breathe out.

2

3 Slowly stretch the arms wide in the next in-breath. Hold and then bring the arms back, breathing out. One more inhalation and then lower them as you breathe out.

LOWER BACK PAIN

CHECKING YOUR POSTURE

It is said that 90 percent of lower back pain is caused by poor posture. It may be felt that this is due to a weakness in human anatomical construction: it is more likely that the cause is a response to present day tensions.

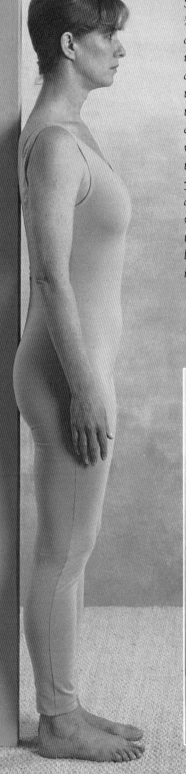

Stand against a wall, with the heels about ¾ inch away from it. Make sure both buttocks and shoulders are touching the wall. Then, using the thumb and forefinger of one hand as a measuring gauge, check the distance between the back of the head and the wall. It should be the same as the heels. You will quite likely find either the head is pressed firmly against the wall, or the gap is considerably greater. Adjust the head to the ¾-inch measure, ensure that you are breathing effectively and then walk around the room. It may well feel odd, but you will now have upright posture. Come back to the wall and check again. It may take quite a long time to correct the posture effectively, but it is important to work at it.

Exaggerating the arm movement slightly, march on the spot or around the room, bringing the knee up and swinging the opposite arm at the same time. Feel the breath adjust itself to the activity. This movement requires a comfortably upright posture and it can help to correct faults.

FORCE OF GRAVITY

*Most people tend to forget that through gravity their bodies are continually
subjected to a downward pressure. This can enhance the problems caused by
incorrect posture. Fortunately you can counteract these bad effects of gravity with
the use of breath and muscles to stretch upward.*

A simple, but highly effective, yoga posture is
called the Palm Tree.

A lying posture, the Scissors, is also valuable.

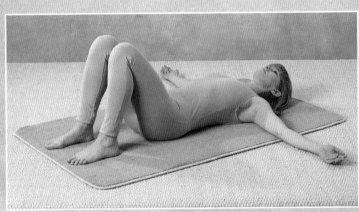

1 Lie on your back, legs bent, the arms streched out to the side,
palms up. Breathe quietly for two or three minutes.

2

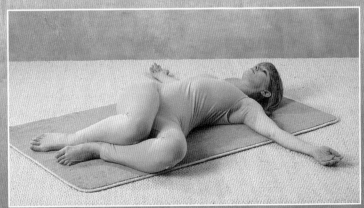

*Stand with the feet a little apart – at the width
of the thighs. Breathe out and, as you breathe
in, spread the arms slowly to the side, bringing
them up over the head until they come straight
up into the air. Stretch as high as you can,
retaining the breath for several seconds. Then,
as you breathe out, bring the arms down again
to the side. Repeat several times.*

2 As you breathe out, bring the knees toward the ground on one
side, keeping shoulders and arms against the ground. Bring the
knees up again on the in-breath and repeat on the other side. Do this
a number of times. Never force the movement, but let the muscles
stretch slowly. Always listen to your own body.

ARTHRITIC CONDITIONS

COUNTERING THE EFFECTS

Arthritis is all too common and can be intensely disabling. It cannot be considered at any depth in this book, but the central contention must be stressed: efficient breathing, linked to a calm mental approach, will ensure the most effective flow of energy through the body, thus countering the debilitating effects.

1 Stand, or sit, with the arms by the side. After an outbreath, bring the arms up to the side, breathing in, and place the fingertips on the shoulders. Again breathe out and, breathing in, bring the elbows back as far as you can, opening the chest.

2 Hold the position for some seconds, then, breathing out, bring the elbows back and continue until they are parallel to one another in front of you. As usual, repeat several times, working just to your current capacity.

THE RIGHT DEGREE OF MOVEMENT

The effectiveness of the breath can be worked on and enhanced at any stage. When this is combined with movement, obviously the degree of movement will be determined by the severity of the condition. However, you should always remember the old adage: "What you don't use, you lose."

1 Sit on the ground, legs stretched out straight in front of you, the arms by the side with the hands supporting your balance.

2 As you breathe out, bring the toes down, stretching the front of the ankles. On the in-breath, bring the toes back toward you, stretching the back of the ankles. Perform this slowly a number of times, again ensuring that you are doing it to your current capacity – not too little, not too much.

3 Bend one leg, placing the calf on the opposite thigh. Steady the leg with one hand and, holding the foot with the other hand, rotate the ankle in each direction. Feel the breath harmonizing with the movement. Alternate between the ankles.

SEVERE FATIGUE

ACHIEVING GENUINE REST

Fatigue can develop to different levels. Often you are not as tired as you believe yourself to be. However, sometimes you really are at rock bottom, but you still need to keep going to beyond the level of your normal resources. At such moments, it helps to assess your mental and physical state and then to take some short-term steps to boost your energy.

When you feel exhausted you are apt to flop into a chair and then attempt to switch off and relax. However, a "flopped" posture can make you feel even more exhausted because your body is constricted. In addition, it is likely that your mind will still be buzzing with problems. An hour or so later, far from feeling refreshed and ready to continue, you will probably still be feeling depleted of all reserves and full of mental turmoil.

1. Heartbeat – too fast and possibly erratic. As the breath slows, with a longer out-breath, be aware of the heart calming and becoming rhythmical.
2. Ribs – rigid from tension. As you work with the breath, they begin to move again. The chest stops heaving and the lower ribs begin to expand and contract.
3. Pressure in head, muscles around eyes, mouth and jaws tense. As breath and muscles relax, pressure eases.
4. Clenched abdominal muscles. Quietly and slowly notice them resume the natural alternation between tension and relaxation.
5. Seized up shoulders and neck. Breathe and relax.
6. Rigidity in hands and fingers. Breathe and relax.
7. Tense feet and ankles and twitching nerves. Breathe and relax.

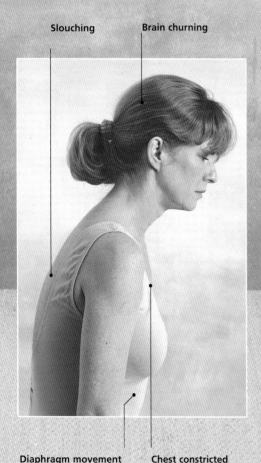

Slouching

Brain churning

Diaphragm movement restricted

Chest constricted

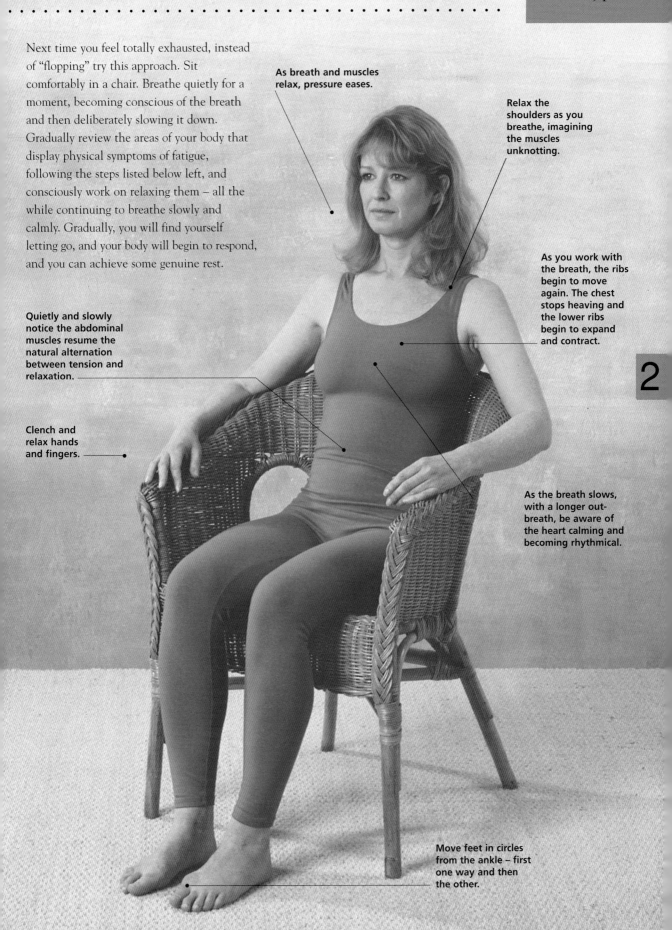

Next time you feel totally exhausted, instead of "flopping" try this approach. Sit comfortably in a chair. Breathe quietly for a moment, becoming conscious of the breath and then deliberately slowing it down. Gradually review the areas of your body that display physical symptoms of fatigue, following the steps listed below left, and consciously work on relaxing them – all the while continuing to breathe slowly and calmly. Gradually, you will find yourself letting go, and your body will begin to respond, and you can achieve some genuine rest.

As breath and muscles relax, pressure eases.

Relax the shoulders as you breathe, imagining the muscles unknotting.

Quietly and slowly notice the abdominal muscles resume the natural alternation between tension and relaxation.

As you work with the breath, the ribs begin to move again. The chest stops heaving and the lower ribs begin to expand and contract.

Clench and relax hands and fingers.

As the breath slows, with a longer out-breath, be aware of the heart calming and becoming rhythmical.

2

Move feet in circles from the ankle – first one way and then the other.

THE COMMON COLD

HEALING AGENTS

If you take the best possible medication, a cold will tend to last for about two weeks, whereas if you just let it run its course, it will be over in about the same time!

Feeling sorry for yourself, you tend to perpetuate the symptoms by failing to ease them. The breath and the touch of the fingers are two valuable healing agents.

1 Sitting comfortably, place the fingers on each side of the top of the nostrils and, on an out-breath, slowly stroke the tips downward in a gentle soothing manner. This can be repeated as many times as seems effective. As with all these measures, keep a handkerchief or tissue near you and do not be concerned about using it as required.

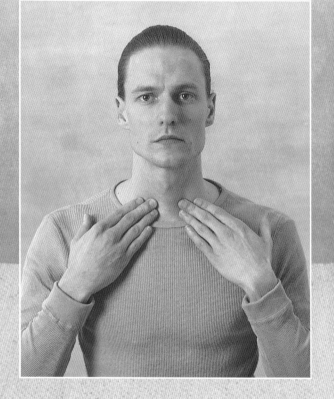

2 Tickles and feelings of congestion in throat and chest can be helped similarly by making stroking movements with the fingertips as you breathe out. Never underestimate the strength of human response to a stroking touch. Likewise, do not expect miracles!

3 Simple, slow, controlled movements of the head can have a clearing effect. Breathing-in slowly, tilt the head as far back as you comfortably can. Never force the movement. If possible, hold for a few seconds in the extreme position.

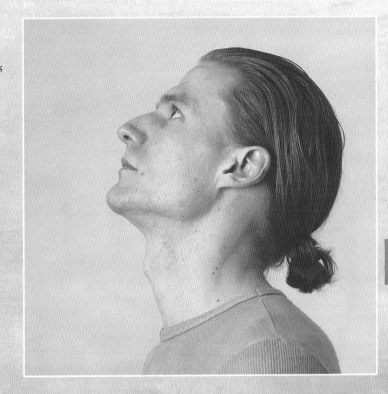

2

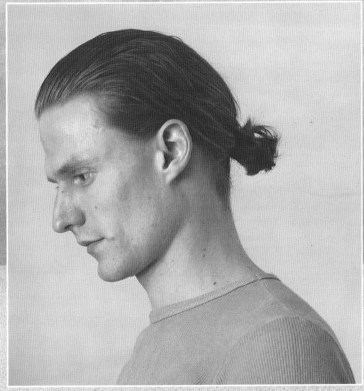

4 As you breathe out, bring the head back, if possible bringing the chin to the chest. The degree to which these movements can be carried out with comfort will vary – listen to your body and go with the moment.

EYESTRAIN

FOCUSING EXERCISES

Most people have problems with their eyes as they get older. It is probable that if they undertook suitable exercises at an early stage, they could effectively delay degeneration. Most, however, wait for the problems to appear before trying to do anything about them.

Focusing exercises can be useful. The value of the breath here may not be apparent, but naturally effective breathing affects the condition of the eyeballs, especially if you link it with a visualization of warm energy flowing into the eyes.

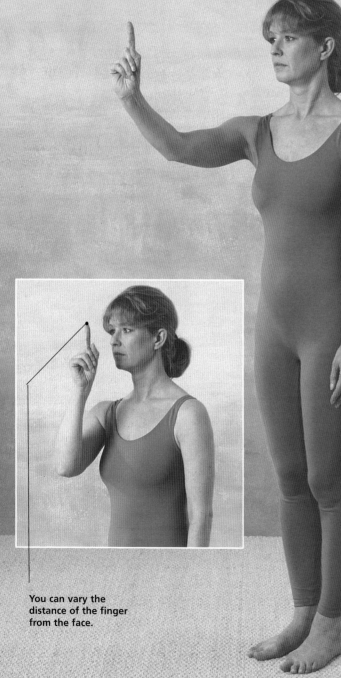

You can vary the distance of the finger from the face.

1 Hold your finger, say, four inches in front of you and focus on it. Then suddenly switch the focus to the wall behind. Continue this quite rapidly, speeding up the breathing at the same time.

2 After such a session, rub the palms of the hands together vigorously, creating heat and then place the hands over the eyes for a minute or two. As this happens, slow the breathing considerably, feeling the warmth from the hands penetrating the eyes.

IMPROVING CIRCULATION

INCREASING RESISTANCE

In many ways people let their circulation become sluggish, resulting in decreased resistance and an increased susceptibility to cold. If you are careful to relate the activity to your physical condition, running, jogging and swimming can be helpful, but you can also achieve a great deal sitting in a chair.

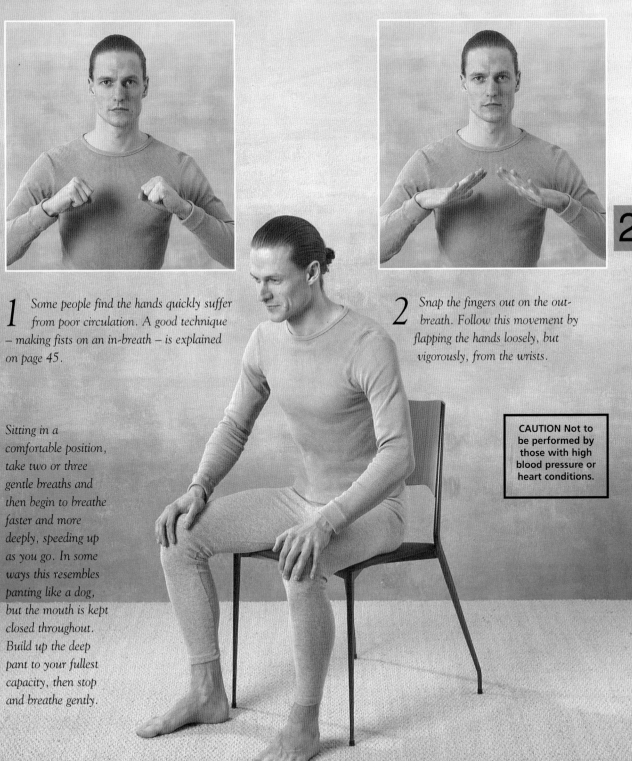

1 *Some people find the hands quickly suffer from poor circulation. A good technique – making fists on an in-breath – is explained on page 45.*

2 *Snap the fingers out on the out-breath. Follow this movement by flapping the hands loosely, but vigorously, from the wrists.*

Sitting in a comfortable position, take two or three gentle breaths and then begin to breathe faster and more deeply, speeding up as you go. In some ways this resembles panting like a dog, but the mouth is kept closed throughout. Build up the deep pant to your fullest capacity, then stop and breathe gently.

CAUTION Not to be performed by those with high blood pressure or heart conditions.

DIABETES

PROMOTING ABDOMINAL HARMONY

Whatever may be the cause of diabetes, an important factor in seeking to restore efficient working of the pancreas is by promoting abdominal harmony.

If you have a machine whose engine is beginning to stutter and that has lost its rhythm, you know trouble is on the way. Abdominal problems create a tension and "stuttering" in the breath, intensifying the difficulties.

The process of sitting on the heels, swinging backward and forward in harmony with the breath and raising the arms away from the back, as described on page 76, is also among those movements beneficial for diabetes. The strong breath, conjoined with the muscular tension and release, massages the abdominal organs, including the pancreas.

Lie on the stomach, feet somewhat apart with the toes outward. Bring one hand round to grasp the opposite shoulder; now do the same with the other hand and drop the head to rest between the bent elbows. Begin to breathe quite deeply but rhythmically; in this instance pressing the abdomen firmly against the floor as you do so. Continue this for two or three minutes, making a balance between strong pressure and total release. Finish by taking several gentle breaths before rising. This is the finest way of developing a balanced pressure/release process on the abdominal organs, including the pancreas.

EPILEPSY

THE BODY'S ELECTRICAL SYSTEM

Epilepsy involves a build-up in the body's electrical system and an attack is, in effect, the body's way of blowing a fuse. You need, therefore, to encourage the maintenance of a steady electrical flow and to avoid overloading the circuit. There is, of course, no "quick fix." This calming approach complements normal medical treatment – it is not an alternative.

The control of the breath with the use of the hands, as shown on page 62, is extremely useful. The fingers can help to enforce a rhythm, for the electrical build-up to an attack will also be accompanied by an increasing breathing tension. Accompanying this manipulation of the breath must be a strong emphasis on evenness of flow: a very calm sea, for example, with rippling harmonious waves, gently moving in and out.

Having used this vision of harmony and even flow while specifically working with the breath, the imagery can also be used on its own, for once sufficiently directed, the breathing pattern will follow the image. This can be achieved with the eyes either open or closed, providing the impression of a rhythmical flow is strongly maintained.

2

RESISTING CANCER

SENSE OF STILLNESS

In recent years more is being heard of doctors who fight cancer by means of the mind, rather than surgery or chemotherapy. In the U.S. Dr. Carl Simonton has worked in this way for years; similar work was pioneered in Australia by Dr. Ainslie Meares.

Insufficient emphasis has been placed on the fact that a calm mind and calm breath go hand in hand. Human beings have a wonderful advantage in their ability to take control of the breathing process to benefit thought and health.

Visualization, with the accompanying restorative breathing pattern, can take countless forms and it is important to find one that appeals, for only in this way can a sufficient depth of concentration be achieved.

There is also no reason why the breathing/visualization process of opposing cancer should not, in many instances, go hand in hand with orthodox medical techniques. As Dr. Bernie Siegel, the American cancer surgeon says, the important thing is to go with the treatment or treatments you are having.

Many people find that they can visualize a rose. Choose a single, beautiful flower of whatever color you wish. Seek to identify wholly with the beauty and the sense of peace that a rose can provide. The rose is not swaying in the wind, but is virtually still. As you absorb its beauty a sense of stillness affects your breathing, that becomes peaceful – but not shallow – and even. This deep sense of harmony in turn stimulates the body's immune system, increasing the effectiveness of its function. Achieving a perfect union takes practice.

Visualization can best be achieved either in a correct sitting position or lying in relaxation.

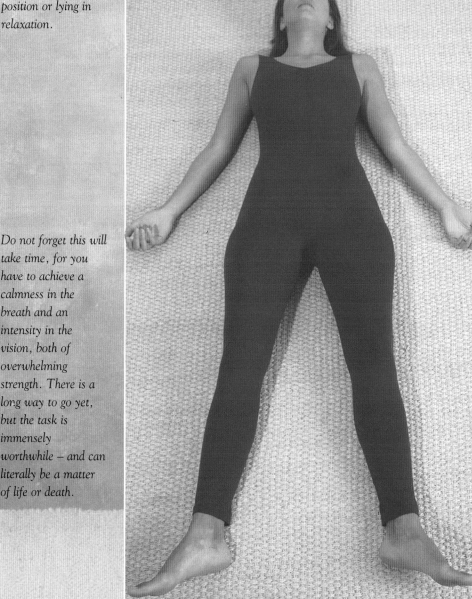

2

Do not forget this will take time, for you have to achieve a calmness in the breath and an intensity in the vision, both of overwhelming strength. There is a long way to go yet, but the task is immensely worthwhile – and can literally be a matter of life or death.

Wherever there may be pain or discomfort, the lying position is best. Remember the knees may be bent if preferred. In this position the breath is freed, the diaphragm can work efficiently and the desired image can be stimulated.

"PUMPING IRON"

INCREASING STRENGTH WITHOUT HARMFUL SIDE EFFECTS

People associate fitness with effort, all too often with veins standing out on the neck and forehead and sweat rolling off the body – some people's idea of "a good workout." Yet statistics show that such effort-bound activities tend to reduce life expectancy and body-builders all too often turn to flab in later life.

When you understand that both physical and mental energy are linked to the breath, and that natural breathing will ensure a free flow of the appropriate aspect of these energies, you realize that all forms of strength are built up by conservation rather than excess.

Try these variations on the yoga Mountain Posture. The effect on muscle tone can be checked by the simple test described on pages 22–23.

1 *Stand with the feet a little apart, the arms by the side. Breathe out quite deeply and, as you breathe in slowly, raise the arms to the side with the hands a little behind the shoulder blades, opening up the chest.*

2 Continue with the in-breath until the
arms are straight up in the air. Then
link the thumbs and stretch upward.
Retain the breath for several seconds.
Now, with a slow out-breath, release
the thumbs and bring the arms back to
the side. Repeat several times.

3

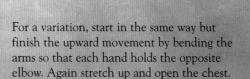

For a variation, start in the same way but
finish the upward movement by bending the
arms so that each hand holds the opposite
elbow. Again stretch up and open the chest.

This posture tenses the whole of the trunk on
the in-breath, only the lower ribs having the
freedom to move. As the arms come down,
the trunk muscles relax and so the classic
pumping basis of strength has been used in a
way that produces no harmful side effects.
After such a breath you can check how much
easier it is to pick up a heavy object.

SPORTING ENERGY

EFFECTIVE EXERCISES

Athletes often go through sequences of exercises similar to those described here. But usually they are performed without special attention to the breath or the mind, both of which are vital to effective exercising.

Body reactions depend to a varied degree on the flow of the breath and calm, controlled thoughts. Exercises performed without mental control produce at best only superficial improvement; at worst they can result in strains and torn muscles.

2 After a couple of minutes stop swinging and simply flop forward, letting the arms dangle. Now focus specifically on the breath, being aware that breathing in involves a slight tension, while breathing out is a release. Concentrate on the out-breath, feeling the muscles relax, especially those in the lower back. Do nothing except let the bend be as free from tension as possible.

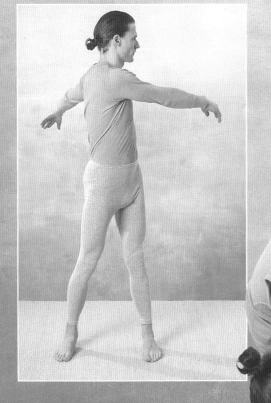

A simple swinging exercise helps to relax taut muscles. Take your time over the whole of this exercise and maintain a calm mental state.

1 Standing with feet apart, swing from the trunk upward, side to side, letting the arms, shoulders and head move freely. Enjoy the sensation of letting go and note how the breath fits into the movement when the mind is involved.

3 Now, as you breathe in, begin to straighten and link the hands behind the back.

4 As you come up, bend the knees a little, thrust the hips forward and swing backward, arms stretched away from the back. Hold for several seconds and then straighten, breathing out.

3

THE BREATH OF SONG

USING THE DIAPHRAGM

*Breathing is a fundamental aspect of singing, both in projecting the voice and in
sustaining the note. Coaches have used a variety of methods in the past, but today
the use of the diaphragm and the control of the abdomen are increasingly
recognized as being of central importance.*

Using the hands to direct the flow of the
breath, as described on page 62, is of great
value to a singer. A common difficulty is
focusing the note through the nasal passages,
rather than the throat.

Using manual control of the diaphragm, via
the ribs, enables more efficient attention to
be given to the flow of the sound. As the
hands can control the length of the out-
breath, practice encourages projection,
eliminating the fear of having to snatch a
new breath too soon.

A neat technique is to hold a lit match or candle quite close to the mouth and then, on the out-breath, to sing a long, sustained note. Control enables the volume and length of note to be maintained without any gusty effect, with the result that the flame does not flicker.

Singers, actors and broadcasters should learn to breathe in through the nose wherever possible. This leads to much more effective voice control and eliminates the unpleasant gasping sound of breathing in through the mouth. Listening to the radio, you will find that you can quickly get irritated by the frequent sound of the mouth in-breathers!

3

SPEAKING IN PUBLIC

EYE CONTACT AND GESTURES

Speaking in public, or conducting important interviews, can be very difficult for many people. Nervousness seizes up body and breath and tension creates devastating rigidity. At best the response will be poor – often it is humiliating.

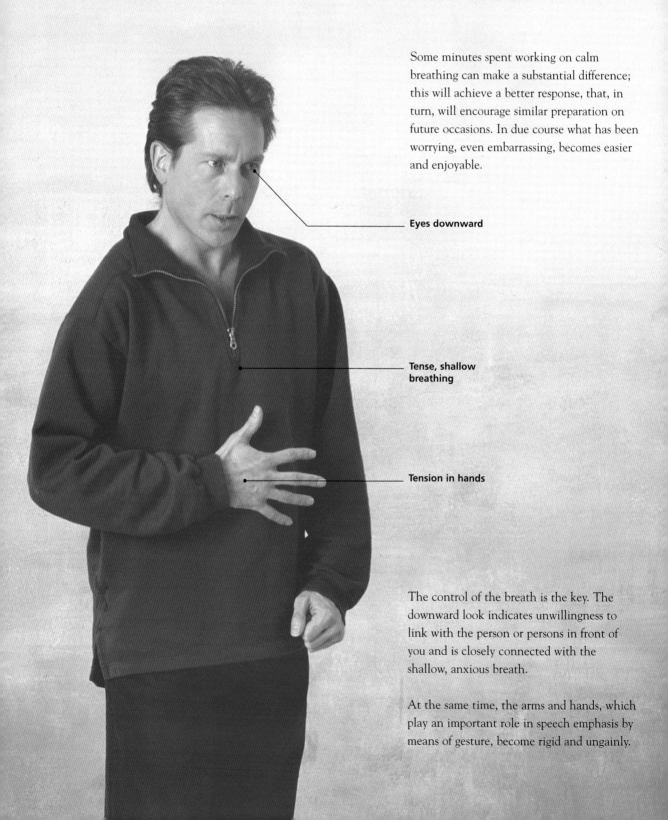

Some minutes spent working on calm breathing can make a substantial difference; this will achieve a better response, that, in turn, will encourage similar preparation on future occasions. In due course what has been worrying, even embarrassing, becomes easier and enjoyable.

Eyes downward

Tense, shallow breathing

Tension in hands

The control of the breath is the key. The downward look indicates unwillingness to link with the person or persons in front of you and is closely connected with the shallow, anxious breath.

At the same time, the arms and hands, which play an important role in speech emphasis by means of gesture, become rigid and ungainly.

When the deeper – in the sense of more thorough – calmer breath has been gained, it becomes more natural to establish eye contact and thereby to involve your audience.

The hands and arms will be relaxed and gestures will become easier and more effective. The back will straighten, establishing an air of confidence.

As with so many aspects of life, the important thing is to be patient. Sweeping changes will not come overnight, but willpower and practice always lead to improvement and thus to success in the long run.

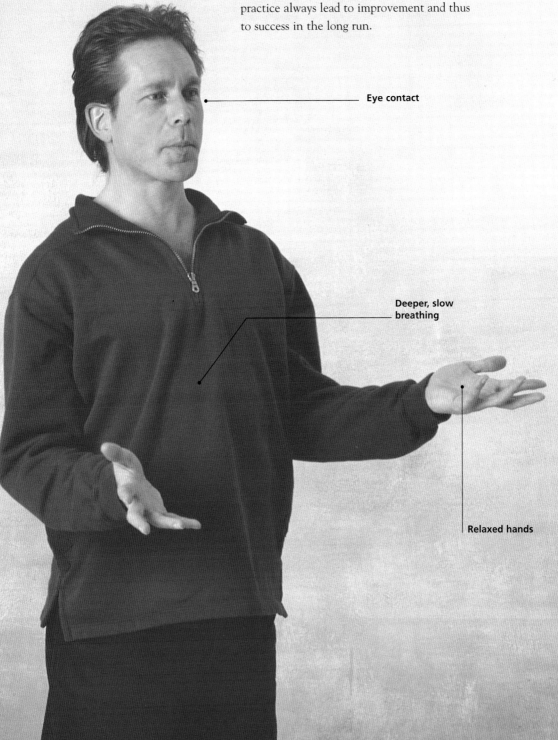

Eye contact

Deeper, slow breathing

Relaxed hands

3

GIVING YOURSELF A
"KICK START"

RESTORING ENERGY

The process of bringing back energy into a tired or depressed body has already been described, but here is a specific technique that can keep you going when it is impossible to let up and take a long break.

This strong technique steps up the circulation and the tension of the muscles sends signals for blood to be conveyed to all parts of the body. This is a powerful form of mental and physical arousal.

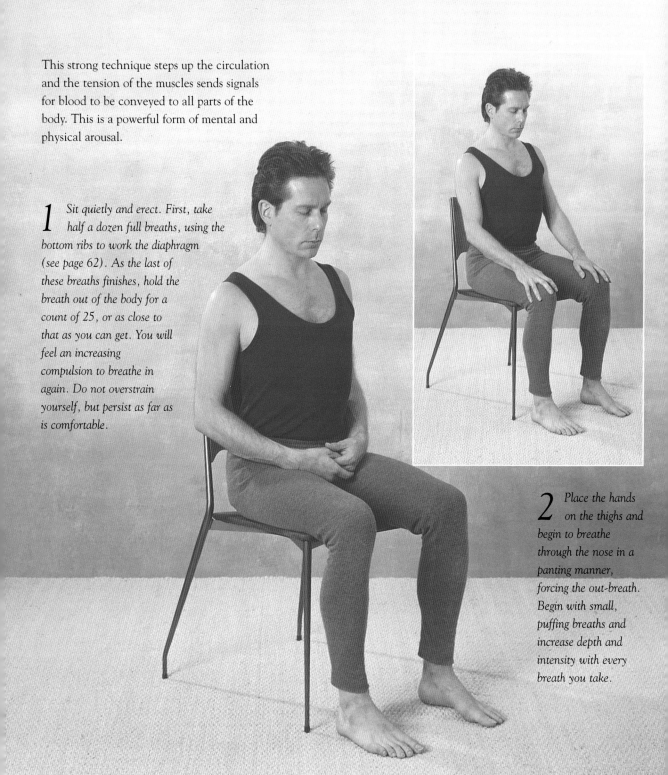

1 Sit quietly and erect. First, take half a dozen full breaths, using the bottom ribs to work the diaphragm (see page 62). As the last of these breaths finishes, hold the breath out of the body for a count of 25, or as close to that as you can get. You will feel an increasing compulsion to breathe in again. Do not overstrain yourself, but persist as far as is comfortable.

2 Place the hands on the thighs and begin to breathe through the nose in a panting manner, forcing the out-breath. Begin with small, puffing breaths and increase depth and intensity with every breath you take.

3 As you do this, tense the whole body –
fingers, hands, arms, toes, feet, legs,
trunk, shoulders, neck and head. Feel all the
muscles tightening. Let the pant rise to a
crescendo and then stop sharply. Hold the breath
out for just a few seconds.

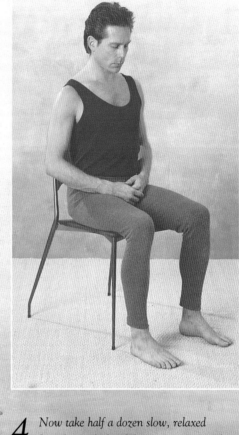

4 Now take half a dozen slow, relaxed
breaths, with the abdomen moving gently.
You will find that you feel full of energy and the
urge to get on and "do."

3

CAUTION This technique is suitable only for
reasonably fit people. The strong pressures
involved can be harmful to some people,
especially those with chest conditions, heart
problems and high blood pressure. If in any
doubt, consult a physician or therapist.

BALANCE IN EVERYTHING

YOGA POSTURES

The understanding of the true role of the breath can make an inestimable difference in your daily life, but the ancient sages of yoga saw also that in the breath lies a key to controlling the mind, which is central to the evolutionary progress of the human being. The fact that breathing is under voluntary control is the most remarkable sign of humankind's development and destiny.

The *asana* – a term now used for a wide variety of postures and movements – was used originally solely for sitting positions, that were said to be firm and comfortable. These positions all involved the correct natural use of the trunk: comfortably upright, the spine balanced, the muscles interplaying effectively, and the diaphragm free to move efficiently.

Most people can manage a simple cross-legged posture, which is quite effective. A cushion may be placed under the buttocks with advantage.

The best-known of these positions is the Lotus, in which each foot is placed upon the opposite thigh. Children do this easily but, as adults let themselves stiffen up, it becomes more difficult. It will be possible with practice, but must never be forced. Always remember the limitations of the knee joint.

Sitting on the heels also permits effective posture. The muscles of the feet and ankles will soon stretch, with practice, to make the position quite comfortable.

Sitting on a chair is also suitable, providing the posture is maintained. The backs of many chairs are badly designed, causing a harmful slouch.

With the body used naturally – when walking, just as much as sitting –
a calm mind will link with calm breathing, each promoting the other.
A yoga student relates that one day he was walking with his master in
London's Piccadilly Circus. He turned and said: "O! Swamiji, if only
now we were in the peace of your ashram in the Himalayas." The
master smiled and replied: "Only when you can find peace in
Piccadilly Circus will you truly find the peace of the ashram."

Our need in life is to find peace and the means of effective action in
whatever circumstances we may find ourselves. The yogis devised a
series of breathing disciplines, which they called *Pranayama* (literally,
"control of the life force") to promote the necessary progress
(see pages 112–121).

4

LOCKING IN THE AIR

CLARIFYING AND CONTROLLING THE MIND

*The process of halting the breath briefly is called Kumbhaka. This can be
practiced after having taken a full breath in, having taken a full breath out, or
indeed at any time, irrespective of the state of the breathing.*

The importance of halting the breath is
evident from the fact that, if you find yourself
in a state of emergency, you immediately and
automatically hold your breath. This clarifies
the mind and helps you to take a split-second
decision. Conscious control is an extension of
this natural process.

*1 The most commonly practiced form of
retention is after having breathed quite
deeply in. Sitting correctly, breathe out and
then take a deep, slow in-breath. Then drop the
chin on the chest, so that it is resting on the
jugular notch.*

2 Retaining the breath, let the abdominal
muscles relax and feel as though you are
sitting on a cushion of air. Avoid any rigidity in
the body.

3 Be aware at all times that you are in
control. There is no need for tension or
anxiety. Let the mind dwell on a single positive
concept – the word "Peace," for example, or a
feeling of a warm, calm day. Sensory messages
will begin to bombard the brain, urging you to
breathe out and take another breath. As soon as
these become strong, obey them in a controlled
fashion, lifting the chin and breathing out slowly.
Initially, you may feel a little dizzy; this is caused
by lack of practice and will soon fade away.
When this occurs, resume breathing again. While
working to retain the breath for longer periods
(ranging from 30 seconds to two minutes), do
not try to prove anything. There is no breath
retention championship!

CAUTION Practices such as this should be
attempted only after effective natural
breathing has become a part of your life.
People with chest or heart conditions, or
those suffering from hypertension, should
not attempt them. Remember at all times to
relate to your body and to work within its
current limits.

4

RESTRAINING THE BREATH

PATH TO MIND CONTROL

Holding the breath out of the body is another aid toward achieving the concentration and clarity that lead to mind control. However, it is essential to see these disciplines are tools rather than challenges. Any sort of competitive spirit or grim determination will be counter-productive.

You have already seen the tremendous differences in the heart's response to frustration and appreciation (see page 82). The electrical signals within the brain also respond in a similar pattern, and so these techniques are used to balance the flow of energy in brain and body.

1 When holding the breath out, after an in-breath, let the exhalation be slow and controlled, drawing in the abdominal muscles to push up the diaphragm, getting as much air as possible out of the lungs. You can never empty the lungs and it is harmful to try too forcefully.

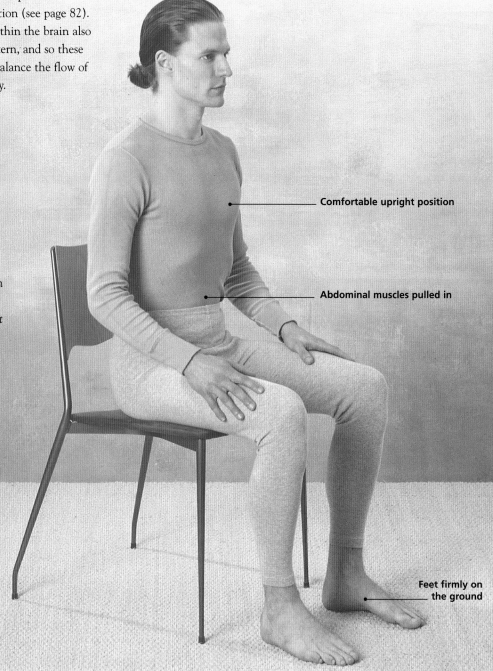

Comfortable upright position

Abdominal muscles pulled in

Feet firmly on the ground

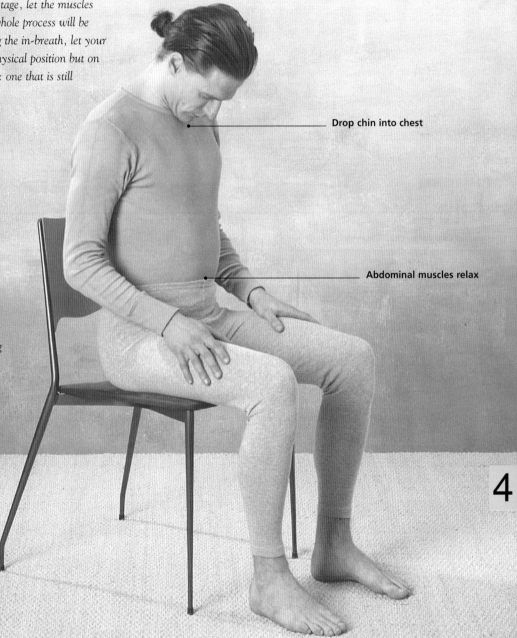

CAUTION Practices such as this should be
attempted only after effective natural
breathing has become a part of your life.
People with chest or heart conditions, or
those suffering from hypertension, should
not attempt them. Remember at all times to
relate to your body and to work within its
current limits.

2 As the exhalation is completed, drop the
chin on the chest and let the abdominal
muscles relax, while still keeping the breath out of
the body. Do not, at this stage, let the muscles
remain too tense, or the whole process will be
negated. As with retaining the in-breath, let your
mind dwell not on your physical position but on
a calming positive thought: one that is still
and reassuring.

3 The period of
holding the breath
out of the body will be
appreciably shorter than
that of holding it in.
Again, respond to the
strength of the sensory
impulses when judging the
time for the next in-
breath. Do not perform
the retention or restraining
exercises for more than
two or three times.

Drop chin into chest

Abdominal muscles relax

4

THE SOUNDING BREATH

ENHANCING THE FLOW

One of the oldest of yoga Pranayama *techniques is called Ujjai, which can be interpreted as meaning "pronounced loudly." This refers to partial closure of the glottis, both while breathing in and out. It results in a controlled sound, like a sob or a moan.*

The purpose of most Pranayamas is to control breath flow, using it to the greatest effect; Ujjai is one process that actually increases the inhalation of oxygen.

Breathe in through
both nostrils

Chest still

Abdomen slightly
contracted

1 Standing or sitting, the important point is the erectness of the trunk. Breathe in through both nostrils, with the glottis partially closed. Ensure the sound comes from this area and not from the nostrils. As you breathe in, keep the abdominal muscles controlled and do not let the stomach bulge.

CAUTION Practices such as this should be attempted only after effective natural breathing has become a part of your life. People with chest or heart conditions, or those suffering from hypertension, should not attempt them. Remember at all times to relate to your body and to work within its current limits.

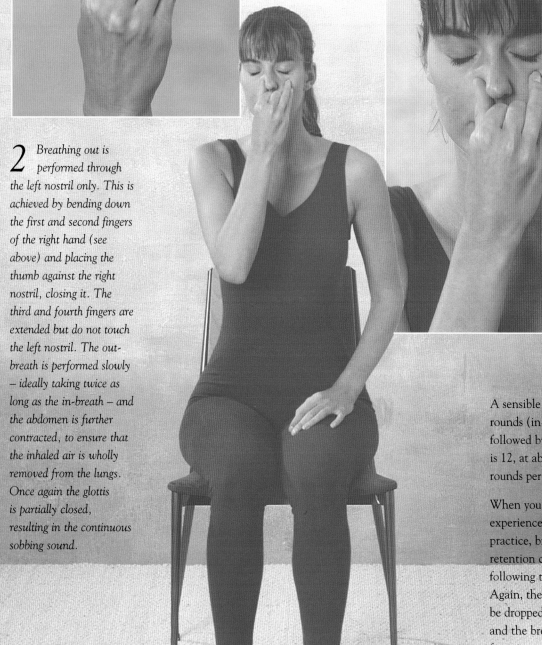

2 Breathing out is performed through the left nostril only. This is achieved by bending down the first and second fingers of the right hand (see above) and placing the thumb against the right nostril, closing it. The third and fourth fingers are extended but do not touch the left nostril. The out-breath is performed slowly – ideally taking twice as long as the in-breath – and the abdomen is further contracted, to ensure that the inhaled air is wholly removed from the lungs. Once again the glottis is partially closed, resulting in the continuous sobbing sound.

A sensible number of rounds (in-breath followed by expiration) is 12, at about four rounds per minute.

When you are experienced at this practice, breath retention can be added following the inhalation. Again, the chin should be dropped on the chest and the breath held in four times as long as the period of inhalation.

4

CLEARING THE HEAD

REVERSING THE BREATHING PROCESS

*Kapalabhati means the "shining head" or "skull." It is a strong, rapid breathing
process that clears the nostrils and, as a result, stimulates the whole head area.
Nasal problems are virtually endemic in contemporary Western society and
therefore this particular technique, while stimulating mental activity also has a
great therapeutic value, if it is worked up to cautiously.*

The effect is achieved by
reversing the normal breathing
process – in the same way as
hearty laughter does. Instead of
drawing the air in through
muscular contraction and then
letting it flow out again, with
Kapalabhati, following an
inhalation, the abdominal
muscles are strongly and sharply
contracted. The mouth is closed
and the air flows through
the nostrils.

This is a rapid breathing process,
with no pause between the in-
and out-breaths – a strong
panting process; in fact, using the
nose rather than the mouth. A
normal round will be between 10
and 12 breaths, performed
thoroughly and rapidly. The
abdominal contraction is
extremely important, resulting in
the major movement of the
diaphragm. This can also be
performed standing.

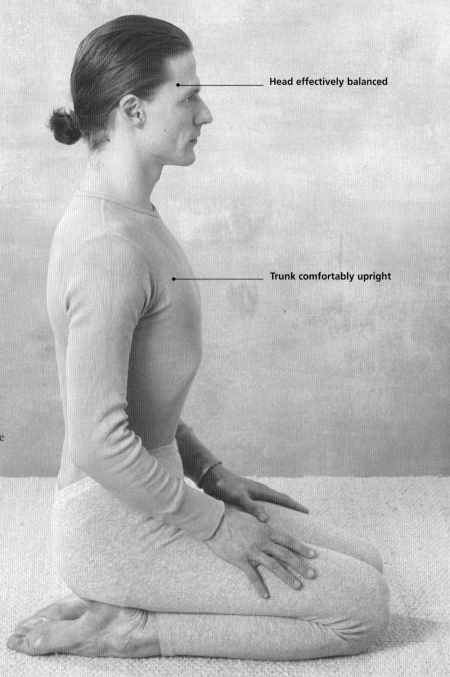

Head effectively balanced

Trunk comfortably upright

When the air flows back into the lungs, the
abdomen relaxes. After one round you should
breathe quietly for, say, 30 seconds, before
starting the next round. About three rounds
will be sufficient at first, building up
gradually. The number of breaths per round
can also be increased with practice.

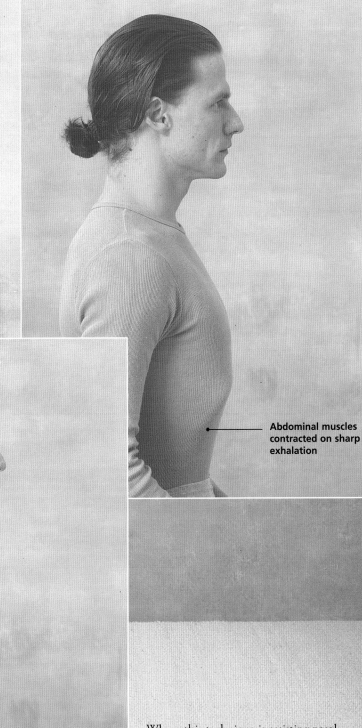

**Abdominal muscles
contracted on sharp
exhalation**

**Abdominal muscles
relaxed on slow
inhalation**

4

Where this technique is assisting nasal
blockages, it is important to have a
handkerchief or tissue near, using it as
required. The strong abdominal movement
also assists the functioning of the organs in
this area (for example, the kidney, liver,
spleen and pancreas).

BLASTS OF ENERGY

· ·

OVERALL BENEFITS

*The Bellows Breath – Bhastrika is the Sanskrit word for a bellows – is similar to
the "Shining Skull," but the small differences are significant and affect the whole
body. The use of the word "bellows" suggests the all-over effect.*

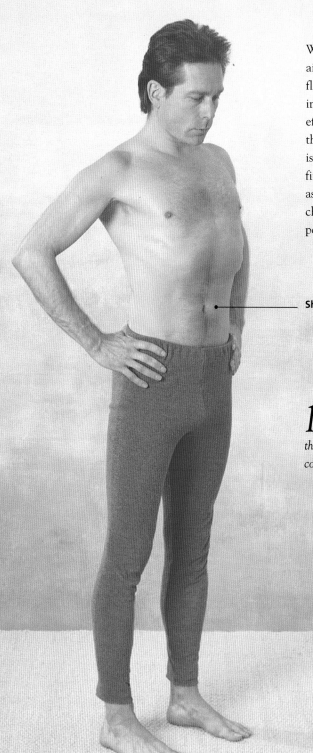

Whereas in Kapalabhati (see page 118) the
air is forcefully ejected and then allowed to
flow back, in Bhastrika both out-breaths and
in-breaths are equally forceful – precisely the
effect of a bellows, in fact. In addition, after
the last inhalation in each round, the breath
is retained as long as possible, before the
final, slow out-breath. The retention is again
assisted by pressing the chin firmly into the
chest. These differences make a standing
position the most suitable for this process.

Sharp out-breath

1 Place the hands lightly on the hips so that
they are not tensed. After a deep in-breath,
the air is forced out sharply by the strong
contraction of the abdominal muscles.

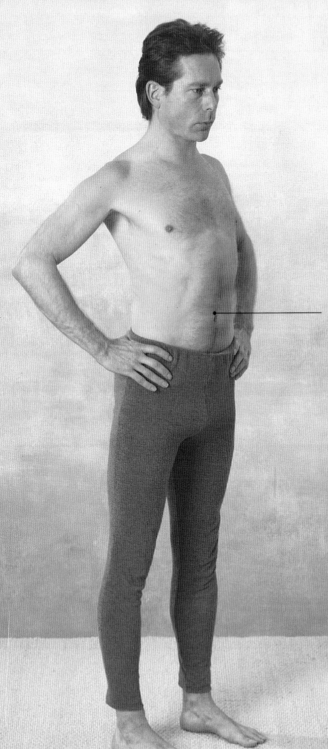

2 *The air is immediately and strongly pulled in again, but without any inflation of the abdomen.*

Strong in-breath

A round is similar to that in Kapalabhati, of 10 to 12 breaths, on the last of which the inhalation is followed by a long retention, with the chin pressed into the chest, with a final, quite slow exhalation. Once again, take a few relaxed breaths between rounds and build up slowly from, say, three rounds as comfort and capacity develops.

It must be understood that while there is a marked similarity, the differences are of singular importance and the resulting effect on the body is dissimilar in a number of ways. With the Bellows Breath the mind should develop an awareness of a flow of energy throughout the entire body.

4

ADJUSTING YOUR BODY CLOCK

MAKING RELAXED BREATHING PART OF YOUR LIFE

The breath is constantly monitoring your state of mind and state of body. It is estimated that normally you take between 14 and 16 breaths each minute, but this figure will vary greatly according to needs at both the mental and physical level.

Throughout this book you will have learned how you can help the breath to work for you, bringing you to a happier state of mind and a healthier state of body.

You will have realized, too, the importance of balance in all things, especially between activation (the "doing" process) and relaxation (the "letting go" process).

True relaxation will always be accompanied by a slowing-down of the breathing process, for the fast, engine-like demand for energy is being stilled, to let peacefulness take over gradually.

When you are in a relaxed state, your respiration slows down to approximately six breaths per minute. This is a natural pattern, but one that can be forgotten as the stresses and strains of life – both physical and mental – take their toll. As a result of this, many people have not taken a naturally relaxed breath in years.

Take a watch with a second
hand and practice taking
breaths (in and out) that last
10 seconds. This will be a
matter of concentration and
persistence. With the watch as
a guide, breathe in for five
seconds and then time the five-
second out-breath. Do this for
two or three minutes at a time.
At first it will seem difficult,
but the will to get it right
always triumphs. Not before too
long, it will once more become
an established pattern in the
brain and when you relax,
formally or informally, this
peaceful breath can take over.

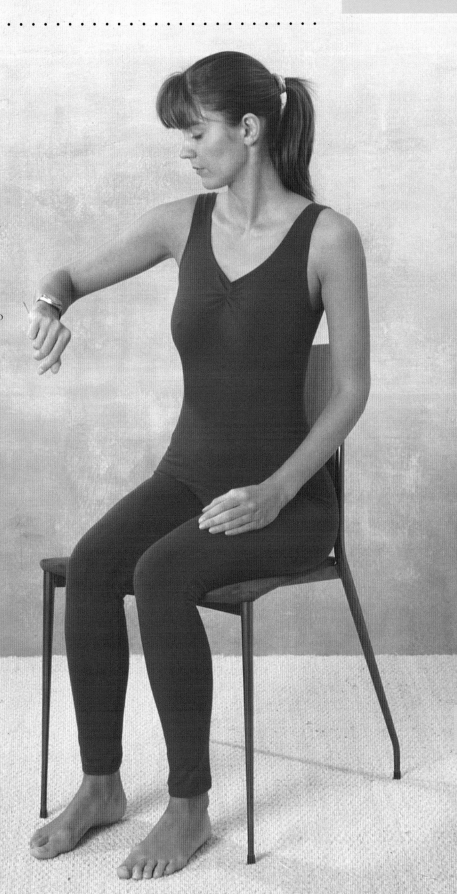

4

While this book shows a wide variety of ways in
which the control of the breath can benefit our lives, it
is important to remember that understanding the basis
of the whole process is the fundamental requirement.
Almost all the specific tips have arisen from this basis.

We all tend to be told what to do, but the truly
rewarding life is one of self-discovery. In this we absorb
that part of the teaching of others that our intuition
tells us is right for us, but we then adapt this to our
own personal needs and it is those little – but vital –
differences between us that are so fascinating.

No day goes by without my spending at least a few
minutes closing my eyes, breathing calmly and saying to
myself as I do so: "I breathe in life/I breathe out life."
From this I truly realize that breath is life; that I have
great control over my breath – therefore I have great
control over my life and my health.

INDEX

ACKNOWLEDGMENTS

All images in this book are the copyright of Quarto Publishing plc
except for those listed below:

Key: a above, l left, r right
Ace 6 (Nasa), 8 (Bill Plummer), 13 (John Searle),25al (Vilbert-Stokes),
80 (John Searle); Harry Smith, 78 br; Giulia Hetherington 111;
Image Bank 35 (Michael Melford), 41 (John Banagan), 52 (L.D. Gordon), 57
(Dan Coffey), 74 (Kaz Mori); Marshall Cavendish Picture Library 69; Safety
in Sport 15.

Quarto would also like to thank the following for supplying
clothing and equipment for photography:

Futon Express
23-27 St. Pancras Road
London NW1 2QB

Dancia International
187 Drury Lane
London WC2B 5QD

This book was designed and produced by
Quarto Publishing plc
The Old Brewery
6 Blundell Street
London N7 9BH

Senior editor Sally MacEachern
Senior art editor Catherine Shearman
Copy editor Alison Leach
Designer Hugh Schermuly
Photographer Paul Forrester
Picture researcher Miriam Hyman
Illustrators Elizabeth Gray, Joanna Cameron,
Halli Verrinder
Background painted by Caroline List
Picture manager Giulia Hetherington
Art director Moira Clinch

With special thanks to the models: Kate Mitchell, Moksaraja, Miles Puffer,
Lynette Wrigley, and to Clare Hayler for her assistance.

The Yoga for Health Foundation operates in many countries and can provide
contacts in others. If you would like further information, please send a stamped,
self-addressed envelope to the Yoga for Health Foundation, Ickwell Bury,
Biggleswade, Bedfordshire SG18 9EF, England.